A new look at the dinosaurs

A new look at the
dinosaurs

Alan Charig, MA, PhD, FIBiol

Curator of Fossil Amphibians, Reptiles and Birds
at the British Museum (Natural History)

British Museum (Natural History)

Colour restorations of dinosaurs by
Peter Snowball

Line restorations by Ray and Corinne Burrows

Book designed by Gillian Greenwood

Published by the
British Museum (Natural History)
Cromwell Road
London SW7 5BD

ISBN 0 565 00883 8

Filmset in Great Britain by
Filmtype Services Ltd, Scarborough
Origination, printed and bound in Italy by
Mondadori, Verona

Contents

Preface

Most of the readers of this book will presumably be interested in dinosaurs, for it is reasonable to suppose that few of those who are not so interested would even bother to open it. It is also probable that many of my readers will be intelligent people with a wide range of interests and a great deal of knowledge on other subjects. Yet I have found that people like that often manage to perform the remarkable feat of going through life without acquiring any real information on dinosaurs whatever – just as I, by contrast, have managed to learn very little of anything else!

In my writing, therefore, I have taken nothing for granted. I have assumed that my typical reader knows practically nothing of dinosaurs or of related matters; or, if he does know something, then what he has learnt is probably wrong or out of date. Long experience has taught me the sort of questions that are most often asked and the sort of misconceptions that are most widely held. This means – if I have succeeded in my intention – that nothing in this book should be beyond the understanding of anyone, and that it should not be necessary to turn to other books for explanation; it should only be desirable, where the appetite for knowledge has been whetted, to look elsewhere for more detailed accounts and (in some cases) different points of view. As for the better-informed reader who finds that he is being told many things that he knew already, I offer him my humble apologies. In any case, he is offered consolation too; the book will doubtless contain a few items of interest, even for him.

In conclusion, I wish to thank John Attridge (Birkbeck College, University of London), Dr William Ball [Keeper of Palaeontology, British Museum (Natural History)] and Dr Edwin Colbert (Museum of Northern Arizona) for their patient reading of my manuscript and for their valuable comments and criticisms. I should also like to express my gratitude to my wife, Marianne Charig, for typing the manuscript and helping in every way possible.

Alan Charig

'The dinosaur' as generally imagined: *Diplodocus*, from the western U.S.A. Typical length 26 metres.

1 · What *were* the dinosaurs?

'Dinosaurs'. The word conjures up, for most of us, a rather hazy picture of the strange prehistoric creatures of the long distant past. Let us look at this picture – even though, as we shall soon discover, much of it is very far from accurate. Enormous beasts, far larger than any elephant, browse placidly in the steaming swamps of millions of years ago; while others, less massive but equipped with formidable teeth and claws, stalk their unsuspecting prey. They have no enemies – except each other – for what lesser animal would dare to attack such giants?

Nevertheless, in popular legend, the dinosaurs' life of unchallenged supremacy was far from idyllic; they were beset by problems. We tend to think of them as being cold-blooded, like the reptiles in the zoo – snakes and alligators, for example – and therefore not very energetic; they move about very little. When they do move, they are clumsy and awkward. They trip over tree-trunks, falling and breaking their legs. Some are so heavy that, once fallen, they cannot even get up again. They have tiny brains and must therefore be extremely stupid. They need vast amounts of food to keep their gigantic bodies going; but their tremendous weight and clumsiness, their slowness and sluggishness and their stupidity appear to give them little chance of getting it. They cannot run fast enough to catch smaller animals on which to feed and they are not even active enough to find a sufficiency of plants to eat. Soon they are starving. They die, one by one, and eventually all are extinct. Only their bones remain. Now, mounted as skeletons in our museums, they fill us all with wonder at their fantastic size.

This unfortunate story of the dinosaurs and their demise – most of it wildly incorrect – has resulted in the use of the word 'dinosaur' as a term of contempt. It is employed to describe something that is outdated, old-fashioned, perhaps grown too large, too slow and too cumbersome; something that is no longer much use to itself or to anybody else in our modern world, like the great passenger liners of the North Atlantic, the 'Queen Mary' and the

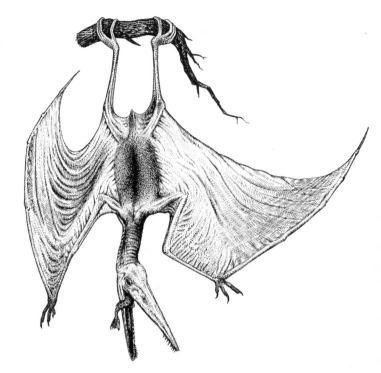

A pterodactyl: *Pterodactylus*, from Germany and elsewhere. Typical wing-span 55 centimetres. *Not* a dinosaur.

'Queen Elizabeth'.

The real dinosaur story, however, is very different from the story that has just been told. Perhaps it should be stated, before going into detail, that not everything in this book will agree with what may be read in other books or magazines or newspapers, or with what may be heard on the radio or seen on television. There are two reasons for this. First, many of the people who write books and articles and scripts for radio and television programmes are not themselves palaeontologists, experts on fossils (although they may style themselves as such!) and they often make mistakes. What is written in one book or programme is generally copied from another; thus, if a book is out of date or simply wrong on certain matters, many others may be too. Secondly, even the professional palaeontologists do not really know very much

A fin-backed pelycosaur: *Dimetrodon*, from Texas. Length up to 3.3 metres. *Not* a dinosaur.

about these strange animals of so long ago. They are still discovering new dinosaurs, finding out more about the old ones, and conceiving new ideas about the way these creatures lived and behaved. What everyone believed to be true twenty years ago is often thought today to be quite wrong. And, on some points, the experts disagree among themselves. Indeed, several lively controversies have arisen in recent years over dinosaurian matters, most of them still unresolved; they are fascinating to follow, especially to the reader who is prepared to take sides.

What, then, *is* a dinosaur? Many people are not at all clear about this and ideas differ considerably. Some of them seem to think that any large prehistoric animal (preferably with an unpronounceable name) is a dinosaur. Dinosaurs, in their view, include not only the familiar *Diplodocus* and *Tyrannosaurus*, *Brontosaurus* and *Stegosaurus*, but also (and in this

they are quite wrong) the fin-backed pelycosaurs, the winged pterodactyls, the great sea-reptiles and even the woolly mammoths. Others believe – and they are equally wrong – that a dinosaur was one, just one, special sort of extinct reptile. Most of those people, if asked what 'the dinosaur' looked like, would probably say that it was an enormous four-legged creature with a very long neck and a small head, standing in the shallow waters of a large lake.

The truth is somewhere in between these two extremes. Dinosaurs are a special group of prehistoric reptiles – we can call them a class or a family if we agree to use those words in a general sense and not with the precise meanings which they have in biological classification; but within that family there were many different dinosaurs. Just as there are many different mammals today (hedgehogs, lions, horses, bats, whales, men) so were there many different dinosaurs – certainly hundreds of

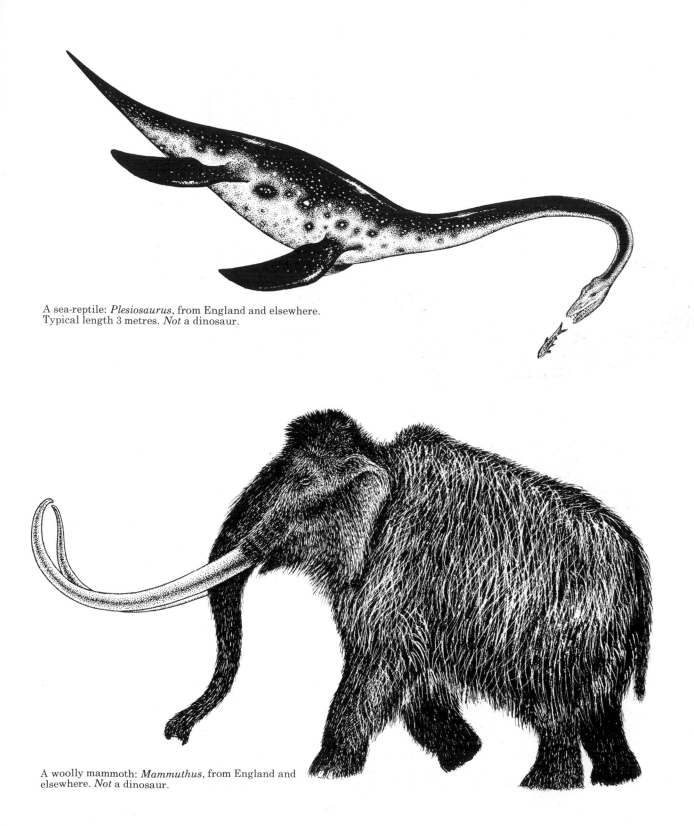

A sea-reptile: *Plesiosaurus*, from England and elsewhere.
Typical length 3 metres. *Not* a dinosaur.

A woolly mammoth: *Mammuthus*, from England and
elsewhere. *Not* a dinosaur.

killing other animals (dinosaurs included). One important difference between dinosaurs and mammals was that all dinosaurs lived on land, although some may have ventured into swamps and lakes. None lived in the sea, and none took to the air – unless we accept the birds as dinosaur descendants, but that is another problem (*see* Chapter 17).

One of the largest dinosaurs known (*Brachiosaurus* from the western U.S.A.; estimated weight 80 tonnes) is confronted by one of the smallest. Some of the little ones were even smaller than this drawing suggests!

A bipedal dinosaur: *Ceratosaurus*, from the western U.S.A. Typical length 6 metres.

different sorts. Some were indeed very large, weighing 80 tonnes or more – as much as twenty large elephants! – but others were quite small; the smallest dinosaur known was no bigger than a mistle-thrush and could have weighed only a few grammes. Some ran around on their hind legs, but others stayed on all fours. Some ate only plants, others, however, ate meat,

Despite their great variety, however, all the dinosaurs – if they are to be regarded as a group – ought nevertheless to have shared at least a few common characters by which that group might be defined. It is accepted that, from a historical viewpoint, the story of dinosaurs began with Gideon Mantell (1790–1852; *see* p.45), the Sussex doctor and amateur geologist

An herbivorous dinosaur: *Anatosaurus*, from western North America, browsing on young trees of the redwood family. Typical length 9 metres.

A quadrupedal dinosaur: *Styracosaurus*, from Alberta. Typical length 5.25 metres.

A carnivorous dinosaur: *Tyrannosaurus*, from western North America, eating a carcass. Typical length 12 metres.

who found teeth and bones in the local quarries in the 1820s; he believed that they represented an entirely new group of animals, the existence of which had not even been suspected until then. They seemed to have been characterized by vast size and herbivorous habits, which – so it was thought in those days – were found together only in certain types of mammals; yet in all other respects Mantell's creatures appeared to have been perfectly good reptiles, and Mantell preferred to regard them as such. His beliefs were confirmed by the great French zoologist Baron Georges Cuvier (1769–1832; *see* p.46), who handsomely admitted in 1824 that he had been wrong in his earlier refusal to accept the reptilian nature of Mantell's discoveries. Mantell's and Cuvier's concept of a group of enormous herbivorous reptiles (a group for

which neither of them suggested a name) must obviously have excluded any gigantic fossil carnivores, of which a few were already known at that time.

In 1841, however, a rather larger grouping was suggested by Richard Owen (1804–1892; *see* p.51), larger not only because of further discoveries made since 1825 but also because this new definition did *not* exclude carnivorous forms. Owen proposed the name Dinosauria for this wider group and defined its members by the characters of their skeletons, some characters resembling those of various other groups of reptiles, others altogether peculiar to the dinosaurians themselves; but he mentioned also their gigantic size, 'far surpassing . . . the largest of existing reptiles' and the important fact that they had lived on land. On the other hand, he did *not* mention the herbivorous habits claimed by Mantell and Cuvier; indeed, the three forms which he cited as the best examples of his new group Dinosauria include one (*Megalosaurus*) which, by the form of its teeth, must obviously have been a highly predatory carnivore. Since

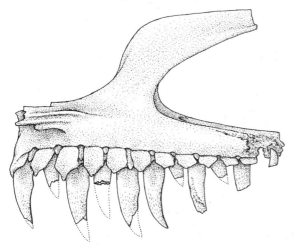

Part of the upper jaw of a *Megalosaurus* skull, from Sherborne in Dorset. The teeth are very definitely those of a meat-eater. Length of fragment 30 centimetres.

Owen's day, therefore, a vegetarian mode of life has no longer been regarded as a necessary attribute of a dinosaur. Nor can large size still be considered an essential dinosaur character, for the remains of many quite small dinosaurs have been unearthed in the last hundred years. Indeed, even the belief that dinosaurs should be classified as reptiles is no longer shared by everyone (again *see* Chapter 17).

Thus all three of the diagnostic characters on which the Mantell–Cuvier recognition of the group was based have now been jettisoned, or are at least doubted by some. It is still believed that dinosaurs dwelt only on land (or, at most, were semi-aquatic in fresh waters); but even that alleged characteristic is not particularly useful in defining the group, for there is no logical reason why some dinosaurs might not have taken to the sea and why, some day, the remains of such creatures might not be discovered. Indeed, it was claimed quite recently (1972) that a small dinosaur from the South of France possessed a paddle-like fore-limb and therefore led a partly heron-like, partly penguin-like existence, but the evidence for this

is not at all convincing.

What, then, are we left with in the way of diagnostically dinosaurian characters? In fact, since the late nineteenth century most people have come to believe that the so-called dinosaurs consisted of two separate groups, the Saurischia ('lizard hips') and the Ornithischia ('bird hips'); each group has its own suite of common characters, which will be discussed in Chapter 10 (p.87). There is no doubt that the Saurischia and the Ornithischia are related to each other, both being members of a larger assemblage (the archosaurs or 'ruling reptiles'); if we could go back far enough in time we should doubtless find that both groups were descended from the same ancestor, itself an archosaur (*see* Plate 17), just as in our own family trees we find that second cousins share the same great-grandfather. But the Saurischia and the Ornithischia may not be *more* closely related to each other than they are to certain other groups of archosaurs which are *not* regarded as dinosaurs – such as the crocodiles and the pterosaurs. (To pursue our analogy further, the second cousins just mentioned may be of similar appearance, tall and blond perhaps, yet each may have closer relatives – first cousins or even brothers and sisters – who are not tall and blond.) There is, as yet, no evidence to suggest that the common archosaurian ancestor of the Saurischia and the Ornithischia – the common ancestor of all dinosaurs – was ancestral to dinosaurs only and not also to those other, non-dinosaurian archosaurs. In other words, the 'Dinosauria' have not yet been shown to form a natural group, and it may well be that they never will – for the simple reason that the natural group in question may not have existed!

Most of the characters which are to be found both in saurischians and ornithischians are, therefore, characters common to the skeletons of all archosaurs (found also, for example, in crocodiles) or distributed more widely still (perhaps in *all* reptiles). Although these archosaur characters are generally rather too technical to be listed here, some of the more important might be mentioned. These include the typical pattern of 'windows' in the sides of the skull; this, in extreme cases, produces a skull which is more like a scaffolding than a solid structure and doubtless accounts for the unusually high

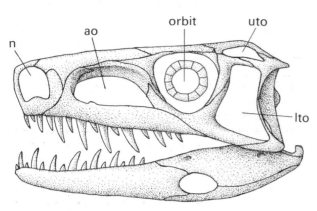

The skull of an early archosaur, *Euparkeria* from South Africa. Length of skull about 8 centimetres.

n	nasal opening
ao	antorbital opening
uto	upper temporal opening
lto	lower temporal opening

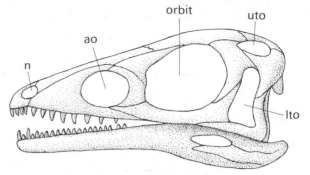

The skull of the dinosaur *Compsognathus*, from Germany. Length of skull as preserved 10 centimetres.

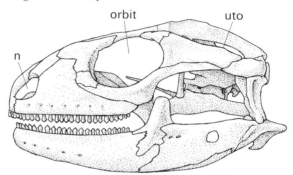

The skull of a lizard (*Cyclura*). Length of skull 6 centimetres. The bony bar beneath the lower temporal opening has been lost.

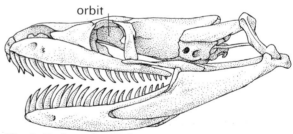

The skull of a snake (*Python*). Length of skull 7.5 centimetres. The bony bar separating the two temporal openings has also been lost.

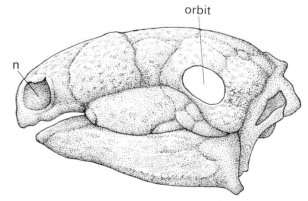

The skull of the dinosaur *Panoplosaurus*, from Alberta. Length of skull about 35 centimetres. All the openings have been secondarily closed.

percentage of archosaur fossils in which the skull is broken into small fragments or missing altogether. Characteristically there are four large openings on either side. The largest, the *orbit*, houses the eye; behind the orbit lie two *temporal openings*, one above the other, which allow for the bulging of the jaw muscles when they contract and probably serve to lighten the skull; and in front of the orbit is an *antorbital opening* which may have contained a gland, perhaps a salt gland. The two temporal openings are characteristic of an even wider subdivision of the reptiles called the diapsids (*see* Chapter 10, p.86), but the additional antorbital opening indicates very definitely that the diapsid possessing it is, more specifically, an archosaur. Further, the bony bars between and surrounding these openings are never reduced or lost in archosaur reptiles, as they are in some non-archosaur diapsids (such as lizards and snakes). On the other hand, in later, more advanced archosaurs some or all of these openings (except, of course, the orbit) may become secondarily closed.

The rest of the archosaur skeleton, behind the skull, is also possessed of some distinguishing features. The fore-limbs are nearly always much

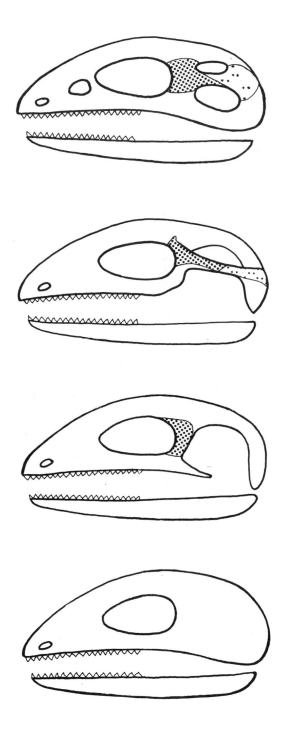

Diagrammatic representation of the same four skulls. Dense stippling postorbital; light stippling squamosal.

shorter and more lightly built than the hind limbs, the front feet are much smaller than the hind feet and may be adapted for grasping, and the tail is large and heavy. There is no doubt that many archosaurs could walk on their hind limbs alone; indeed, some had fore-limbs so small or so thoroughly adapted to grasping that they must have been quite useless for walking and the animal must therefore have been obliged to employ a bipedal gait at all times. (*Tyrannosaurus* is a good example; *see* figure on p.14 and Plate 18.)

Because of this it has generally been assumed that the unequal limbs and heavy tail suggest a strong tendency towards bipedality in *all* archosaurs, right from the very beginnings of their history, and that even those archosaurs which were entirely quadrupedal were nevertheless descended from bipedal ancestors. Since about 1961, however, this idea has been regarded with ever-increasing scepticism – mainly because, in most cases, there is nothing in the structure of the quadrupedal archosaurs (limb length and tail apart) to suggest that they had evolved from bipeds and that, in consequence, they were only secondarily quadrupedal. Rather is it thought that the disparity of the limbs and the powerful tail evolved originally in connection with some other function (one possibility put forward is that the ancestral archosaurs were semi-aquatic) and that those same characters made it easier for the animals to raise their front feet off the ground and walk bipedally.

It is true, then, that many dinosaurs of both groups were of gigantic dimensions, that many were herbivorous, and, moreover, that many were bipedal. Unfortunately none of these characters can be used as a dinosaurian diagnostic, for, as already mentioned, it is also true that many of these creatures were of modest size, that many were entirely carnivorous and that many were always quadrupedal in their habits. (Nor is any of those characters even limited absolutely to either group; but only one apparently carnivorous ornithischian is known, *Troodon*, unearthed in Montana as recently as 1980.) We therefore ask: can we find *any* simple feature absolutely diagnostic of dinosaurs, present in all of them – saurischians as well as ornithischians – but lacking in every other reptile?

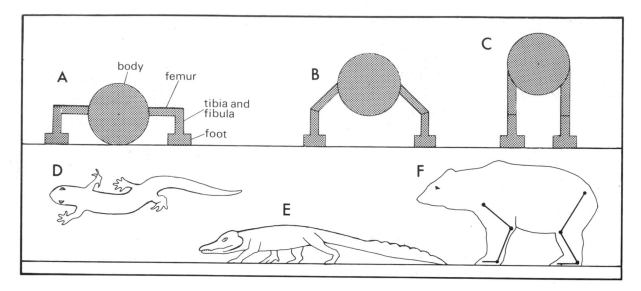

Limb posture and locomotion in four-legged vertebrates:
(a) A 'sprawler', such as a lizard.
(b) A 'semi-improved' animal, such as a crocodile in a hurry.
(c) A 'fully improved' animal, such as an advanced mammal or a dinosaur.
(d) A 'sprawler' from above – a newt – showing the horizontal S-shaped waves.
(e) A 'semi-improved' animal – a Mississippi alligator in a hurry – raised clear of the ground.
(f) A 'fully improved' animal – a bear – a generalized advanced mammal with its feet flat on the ground.

The answer to that question is 'yes'. All dinosaurs are characterized by a 'fully improved' or 'fully erect' position of the limbs (not unlike that found in higher mammals) in which the limbs support the body from beneath, holding it clear of the ground, and each moves in a more or less vertical plane. This contrasts strongly with the sprawling position of the limbs found in amphibians and most other reptiles – including the earliest archosaurs. Sprawlers rest with the belly on the ground and the upper segment of each limb (upper arm or thigh) projecting sideways from the body; they push themselves forwards by throwing the trunk and tail into horizontal S-shaped waves and pivoting on their limbs – virtually 'swimming' over the land. In the dinosaurs, as in the mammals, the front leg had been swung round so that the elbow projected backwards, not sideways, and the back leg had been swung in the opposite direction so that the knee pointed forwards. An intermediate condition, 'semi-improved' or 'semi-erect', is found in other archosaurs, in particular in those immediately ancestral to the dinosaurs and in crocodilians. (Modern crocodiles are normally 'sprawlers' when walking slowly but, when in a hurry, they can lift themselves into the 'semi-erect' position and move in a sort of trot; some even gallop.)

Although the dinosaurs are totally extinct, their 'fully improved' condition is shown very clearly by a whole suite of characters of the bones of the limbs (especially of the hind limbs) and of the girdles – shoulders and hips – to which the limbs attached; the bones were necessarily very different in shape from those of their sprawling ancestors. To mention just a few of the more important differences, the thigh-bone of a dinosaur is fairly straight and has an inturned head, that of a sprawler is slightly S-shaped and has no head. The hip-socket is basin-shaped in dinosaurs as well as in sprawlers; in dinosaurs, however, there is a large hole in the bottom of the basin and a strongly developed upper rim, while in sprawlers neither of those features is present. Dinosaurs walked on tiptoe, but sprawlers padded along on the soles of their feet.

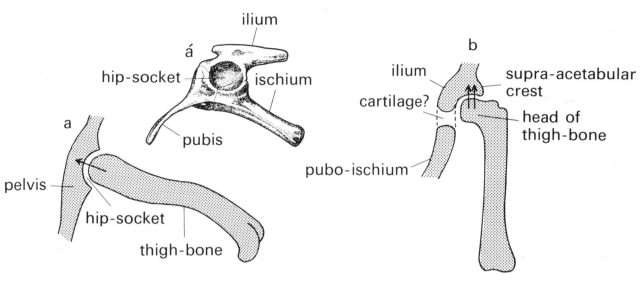

(a) The hip-joint and thigh-bone of a 'semi-improved' reptile. The arrow shows the direction of the thrust of the thigh-bone into the hip-socket. The thigh-bone is slightly S-shaped and has no inturned head; the hip-socket is a complete bony basin, without a strongly developed upper rim.

(a′) The pelvis (hip-girdle) of a fossil reptile, *Ticinosuchus* from Switzerland, which belonged to the group ancestral to dinosaurs. This animal was 'semi-improved' and its hip-socket was complete.

(b) The hip-joint and thigh-bone of a dinosaur. The thigh-bone is fairly straight and has an inturned head; the hip-socket has a large hole in its base.

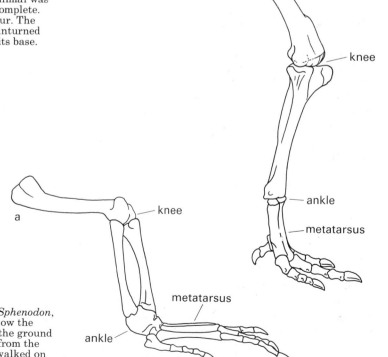

(a) The skeleton of the hind-leg and foot of *Sphenodon*, the New Zealand tuatara (*see* p.37), to show the position of the foot with the sole flat on the ground

(b) The same of the dinosaur *Ceratosaurus*, from the western U.S.A., to show how dinosaurs walked on their toes

These limb 'improvements' were of great significance in the evolution of *true bipedality*. A true biped is one which hardly ever touches the ground with its front legs when running, perhaps never, and which can walk slowly or stand still on its back legs alone. But problems of balance and muscle strain make it impossible for a *sprawler* to run far on its widely splayed back legs alone; modern lizards, for example, are generally compelled to limit their bipedal locomotion to short rapid dashes and could never be described as *true* bipeds. The more a quadruped 'improves' its locomotion by bringing its legs beneath its body and narrowing its trackway, the less effort and energy does it require to keep its body off the ground, both when stationary and when moving, and the more easily can it rear up on its back legs to become a true biped. (The saurischians seem to have carried the trend towards bipedality farther than did their ornithischian cousins; many saurischians were *obliged* to walk on their back legs alone, but it is likely that most, if not all, of the bipedal ornithischians could come down on all fours when they wished.)

Bipedal running in the basilisk lizard, *Basiliscus*, from Central America and northernmost South America

To sum up, it seems that the dinosaurs were the only archosaurs – indeed, the only reptiles – to succeed in acquiring a 'fully improved' stance and gait; and, in consequence, it is only among the dinosaurs – both saurischians and ornithischians – that we sometimes find true bipedality, either habitual or obligatory. These common trends are highly important in that they provide some justification for our use of the popular term 'dinosaur' to cover both groups. At the same time, however, the differing details of the necessary modifications to the animals' skeletons clearly suggest that each group had evolved its own modifications independently of the other. A comparable situation can be imagined where each of two motor-car manufacturers produces high-performance versions of its various standard models by modifying all of them according to the company's patent specification; it is obvious that the two types of modification, although both designed for the same purpose, are bound to be rather different from each other and characteristic of their respective companies.

Let us return to the picture of the dinosaurs that we described at the beginning of this chapter – the cold-blooded dinosaurs of popular imagination, slow, clumsy and stupid and not particularly good at keeping themselves alive. Some scientists now believe that dinosaurs were warm-blooded, like birds and mammals; later in this book (Chapter 16) we shall explain why. Those same scientists also believe that the dinosaurs were *not* all slow and clumsy, that some of them could run very fast and that their legs were suitable for a very active life. Nor is there any reason to suppose that they were any less intelligent than the reptiles of today; it is not so much that their brains were very small, rather is it that their bodies were unusually large in comparison.

In any event, whether cold-blooded or warm-blooded, the dinosaurs as a group lived for about 140 million years. For most of that time they ruled the land; no other animals could compete with them. They could hardly have survived for such a vast period if they had been so slow and clumsy, so poor at the job of making a living. After all, the human race (as defined by the anthropologists) has lived for only a couple of million years or so, four million at the most;

who are we to scorn the dinosaurs when, as a group, they proved themselves able to last for seventy times as long as we ourselves? *Civilized* man, indeed, goes back only a few *thousand* years into the mists of antiquity. Using the word 'dinosaur' in a disdainful manner, as described above, is therefore quite unjustifiable.

On the contrary, the dinosaurs must have been highly successful animals, each well fitted to lead the particular sort of life that it had chosen. None of the different sorts, of course, lasted for the whole of their 140-million-year history. The dinosaurs, like everything else in the living world, were constantly changing; and the dinosaurs of approximately 200 million years ago (the time when they began) were mostly very different from the last of their descendants, whose reign came to a sudden and inexplicable end about 65 million years before the present. (After all, the last of the dinosaurs were nearer in time to *us* than to the earliest members of their own group.) Each period during the Age of Dinosaurs had its own characteristic 'collection' of these remarkable animals.

Today, therefore, the dinosaurs belong to the past; there is nothing but their fossilized remains to show that they ever existed (unless, once again, we accept the birds as their descendants). The general public has nevertheless developed an insatiable interest in dinosaurs over the course of the last hundred years or so; the Dinosaur Gallery is invariably the major attraction of any natural history museum fortunate enough to have one, and the vexed question of the extinction of these extraordinary beasts exerts as perennial a fascination over the layman as over the professional scientist. Another source of popular interest is the story of their discovery in the nineteenth century, first in England and then in North America. So great an interest is more likely to be due to the often gigantic size of the dinosaurs and to their often bizarre appearance than to their historical importance. Yet the latter can hardly be over-estimated, for the dinosaurs undoubtedly played a major part in the shaping of the natural world as we know it; it seems certain that, without them, the whole course of evolution would have been entirely different and man himself would never have originated.

2 · Our changing world

Today there are many different sorts of plants and animals – we call them species – that are quite separate and distinct from each other. They usually breed only with other members of the same species, producing offspring which, when fully grown, look very much like their parents. A cow is a cow, a pig is a pig, and one cannot be crossed with the other to produce something in between. It is true that different breeds of dog can be crossed with each other to produce mongrels, but they are all dogs nevertheless. It is also true that different but closely related species can sometimes be crossed with each other to produce what we call a hybrid (a male donkey and a female horse will together produce a mule), but these hybrids themselves cannot usually breed at all.

This state of affairs, with separate, distinct and apparently fixed species, seems to disprove the observation (made at the end of the last chapter) that everything in the living world is constantly changing. We do not notice the changes, however, because they are taking place so slowly – slowly, that is, in comparison with the seventy years or so that is the average life-span of a human being. Even if we look at the land animals of, say, five thousand years ago, they seem to be much the same as they are at present. But if we look at the animals of five million years ago, they are not the same at all; we can still recognize, for example, lions and horses and monkeys and ostriches, but they are different *sorts* of lions and horses and monkeys and ostriches from those alive today. If we go back fifty million years we find that some of the animals are just about recognizable – we might still see a horse, but it would be no bigger than a fox-terrier, with three or four toes on each foot instead of hooves – and others are so strange that we cannot name them at all in terms of anything familiar. Finally, let us go back a hundred million years. Now we shall find that most of the animals are quite unrecognizable, for we are back in the Age of Dinosaurs; the only familiar backboned animals on the land are turtles and lizards and crocodiles, and even those are rather different from their modern counterparts.

This is true also of flying birds and of fishes, of snails and of worms, of trees and of seaweeds.

An ancestral horse, *Hyracotherium*, from the London Clay (known also as *Eohippus*). About the size of a fox-terrier.

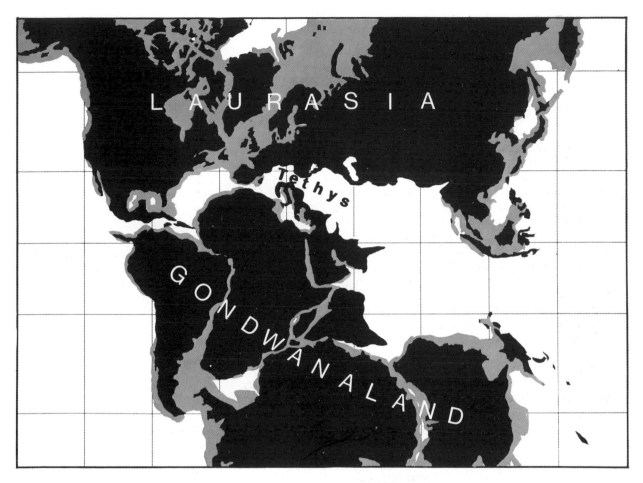

A map of the world as it was 140 million years ago, in Late Jurassic times. The grey areas around the margins of the black continents are the continental shelves, beneath the sea at present but not necessarily submerged at other times.

Nothing, but nothing, remains the same. Everything is evolving. Why living things evolve, and how they evolve, are only partly understood; but alas, a full treatment of that subject is beyond the scope of this book.

As time passes, then, each species – a living, interbreeding population – is undergoing constant change. But an alteration may arise in only some members of that population, a change in their anatomical structure, behaviour or genetical make-up, which somehow prevents them from breeding with other members of the same species living in the same area. Once this has happened, once the individuals with the altered character are *reproductively isolated* from those without it, the 'mixing in' of all the heritable characters of each group with those of the other will stop and the differences between the two groups will probably increase. Thus the evolutionary lineage will have split into two or more branches; the old species will have speciated into two or more new ones. Reproductive isolation comes about all the more easily as a result of geographical isolation; for example, a mountain range may be transformed by a rising sea-level into a chain of islands, so that the animals on each (good swimmers and flyers excepted) are cut off from contact with others of the same species on neighbouring islands. Each group on each island will then continue to change, to evolve, but the groups will not change in exactly the same direction or at the same speed; their differences will gradually increasè until populations from neighbouring islands, were they able to renew contact, would no longer be able to breed together.

It will be understood, of course, that not all species eventually evolve into new ones. A few of the others persist almost unchanged over vast periods of time, but most of them die out completely without leaving any descendants whatever.

We have seen that the living world is changing; but, even more surprising, the non-living world is changing too. Everything on this planet is in a state of flux. Here we must think particularly of the geography and the climate, each affecting the other. The continents are changing shape, drifting apart, coming together and breaking up again. (A map of the world during the Age of Dinosaurs is quite unlike a map of the world today; but then, a movement of 2 or 3 centimetres each year since the last dinosaur perished would amount to 1600 *kilometres* by now.) Mountain ranges are thrust up, others are worn down, islands in the oceans appear and disappear. At some times in the past the earth has been generally warmer than it is today, at other times much colder; the differences between summer and winter have been less marked than at present or absent altogether. Ocean currents flow along differing paths and the rainfall varies enormously. Because of such changes rivers dry up or move their courses, lakes come and go, glaciers and ice-caps advance and retreat, fertile lands become deserts and vice versa.

All these changes, in turn, affect the plants and animals, forcing them to migrate to more suitable parts of the earth's surface or, by evolving, to adapt themselves to the changed conditions. If they cannot do either, they die out. Conversely, the absence or presence of vegetation can affect both climate and geography. Quite drastic changes of this nature can take place over comparatively short periods of time, well within the life-span of an individual man.

The contents of this chapter must seem to be the very opposite of what is written in the Bible, in the first chapter of Genesis. There it tells how God created the earth, and then, in four days, all forms of plant and animal life (including man himself) just as we know them today. Every living thing was created 'after his kind'. Most people, however, no longer believe that the Biblical story of the Creation is literally true. They look upon it as a parable, an allegory (like many of the stories told by Jesus in the New Testament); in other words, it is a fictitious story which serves to illustrate a moral teaching. Many leaders of the Church now accept that the earth and the living things upon it are constantly changing; indeed, some of them have been pioneers of research into evolutionary history. There is no real conflict between science and religion.

3 · How dinosaurs were fossilized

Everything we know about dinosaurs has been learnt from the study of fossils. The word 'fossil', in its widest sense, means anything dug up (Latin *fossilis*, from *fodere* to dig). But now it is nearly always used in a more limited way, to mean the remains or traces of a prehistoric animal or plant, remains that have been buried in the rocks of the earth's crust for thousands or millions of years – even hundreds of millions of years – and turned into stone.

Dinosaurs were vertebrate animals, as are we ourselves; they had skull and jaw, backbone, shoulder-bones and hip-bones, and bones of the limbs and feet. Unlike us, they sometimes had a bony armour on the outside as well. They all lived on land, some perhaps venturing into fresh water – lakes, swamps and rivers – from time to time. Sooner or later they died, of disease or old age or maybe killed by other dinosaurs. Usually the body lay on the ground, where it was quickly eaten by flesh-eating animals; they crushed up some of the bones (if they were not too large!) and scattered them around. If the corpse remained uneaten it just rotted away. Very occasionally the carcass might be saved from destruction by being buried almost immediately after death in shifting sand dunes or in volcanic ash, but in most cases it was left on the surface and before long had disappeared without trace – even the skeleton. On the other hand, when the dinosaur had died near a river or in a swamp it stood a much better chance of being preserved. Its body might sink into the mud on the spot, or flood-waters might

Dinosaur teeth of various sorts. *Above left.* Unworn tooth of *Iguanodon. Above right.* Tooth of ankylosaur. *Below, left to right.* Tooth of Megalosaurus; tooth of sauropod; tooth of *Iguanodon* worn down to chisel-like cutting edge; another *Iguanodon* tooth worn down to flat shearing plane. The *Megalosaurus* tooth is 6.8 centimetres long as preserved.

sweep it into the river to float downstream and end up on a sand-bar, on the bottom of a lake or even in the sea. The flesh would decay and the bones would gradually be covered by the sediments – such as mud or sand – which are always accumulating in such places.

Those sediments (including those formed on dry land from dune sand or volcanic ash) would be buried beneath further layers, and the weight of the layers above would compress them and turn them into rock: mud into clay, sand into sandstone, limy oozes into limestone or chalk. Meanwhile water was seeping through the bones, and the mineral salts dissolved in the water were gradually changing the bones into rock, making them much heavier than before; in other words, the bones were being mineralized or petrified. The mineralization of the bones did not alter their characteristic shapes, but the enormous weight of the overlying rock often squashed them a little – sometimes deforming them very considerably.

At the same time the layers of rock in the earth's crust were moving – rising, sinking, folding and buckling – and were taking the fossil-bearing layers with them. (This too may have helped change the shape of the bones.) What had once been the floor of a lake or of the ocean became dry land, a wide plain or a range of mountains. Then the sea crumbled the cliffs around the shores of the land, rivers cut through the plain, the mountains weathered away; and one day, millions of years after burial, the bones of the dinosaur appeared again in the sea-cliffs or the valley walls or on the sides of the mountain. Sometimes this re-appearance was hastened by the work of man as he dug his claypits and his quarries and his mines, made his cuttings and tunnels for roads and railways or excavated for the foundations of his schools and office blocks.

However, dinosaur fossils are not always bone. Other parts of the animal, or indeed anything that it made – such as droppings or footprints – are fossils too. Very often we find teeth, which are even harder than bone and preserve well. We do not often find skin, but there is sometimes an impression of its outer surface made on the surrounding mud soon after death; in the Natural History Museum in London there is an impression of the scaly skin on a dinosaur's tail. In the same way we do not

An impression of the skin on the tail of a duck-billed dinosaur (*Edmontosaurus*) from the Upper Cretaceous of Alberta

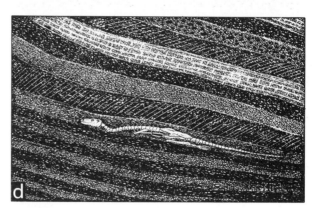

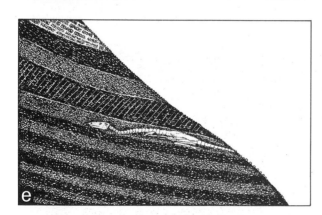

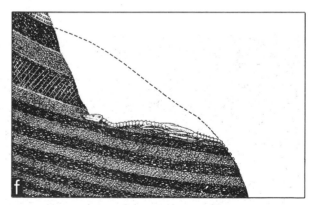

The sequence of events leading to the unearthing of a dinosaur skeleton:

(a) The dead dinosaur sinks to the bottom of the lake.
(b) The flesh begins to decay, gradually exposing the skeleton. Meanwhile the carcass is being covered by sediment.
(c) The flesh has rotted away entirely. Further layers of sediment are accumulating above the skeleton.
(d) Vast thicknesses of sediment have now formed above the dinosaur. Their weight is compressing the lower layers into narrower bands and turning them into rock. The lake has long disappeared. Meanwhile the bones are being both flattened and mineralized.
(e) Internal movements of the earth have lifted the layers in its crust, and erosion is now carving a valley through the strata. Eventually the bones of the tail begin to weather out and roll down the hillside.
(f) Palaeontologists (fossil experts) have noticed the bones and have dug out the overlying rock to expose the complete fossil.

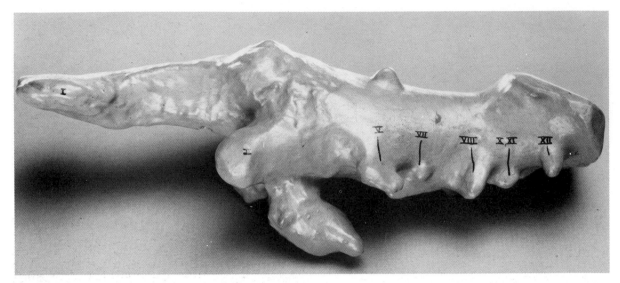

find dinosaurs' brains, but for some dinosaurs we have a cast of the skull cavity, made naturally by the mud that oozed into the hole once filled by the brain. Such a cast is of almost the same size and shape as the brain itself, so it gives us a fairly good idea of how big the brain was and what it was like; it often shows the roots of the cranial nerves. Even the blood-vessels of the head region and, most unusually, the membranous labyrinth of the inner ear with its semicircular canals are sometimes preserved in the same manner. In some dinosaurs there seem to have been large smooth stones (called gastroliths) in the stomach, just as in modern crocodiles; the crocodile, a mainly aquatic animal, swallows them deliberately and uses them not only to grind up its food into smaller pieces but also to adjust its buoyancy in the water. In a couple of dinosaurs the actual contents of the stomach are preserved and have been analysed, so we know what the creatures had eaten just before they died. There are also dinosaur skeletons with (so it seems) the skeletons of unborn young inside the mother; unless, of course, such specimens represent cannibalistic adults which had swallowed the young of their own kind! Fossilized bits of egg-shell (even whole eggs), fossilized droppings and, quite often, fossilized footprints and trackways have all been found abundantly. The difficulty with all of these is that we cannot be quite certain *which* dinosaur laid the eggs, produced the droppings or made

An artificial cast of the brain cavity in the skull of the horned dinosaur *Triceratops*, from the Upper Cretaceous of Wyoming, showing the roots of the cranial nerves (numbered with Roman numerals). Length 15.5 centimetres. The figure on p.74 is a photograph of a *natural* endocranial cast.

Alleged dinosaur gastroliths (stomach stones). The central stone is 7 centimetres long.

A natural cast of the membranous labyrinth of the inner ear of the ornithopod dinosaur *Iguanodon*, from the Lower Cretaceous of Sussex (*see* the figure on p.74). One of the three semicircular canals has been broken and the gap has been repaired with plaster of Paris. Width of entire labyrinth 3.6 centimetres.

Two coelurosaur skeletons (*Coelophysis*) from the Upper Trias of New Mexico, with the bones of smaller individuals within the rib-cages.

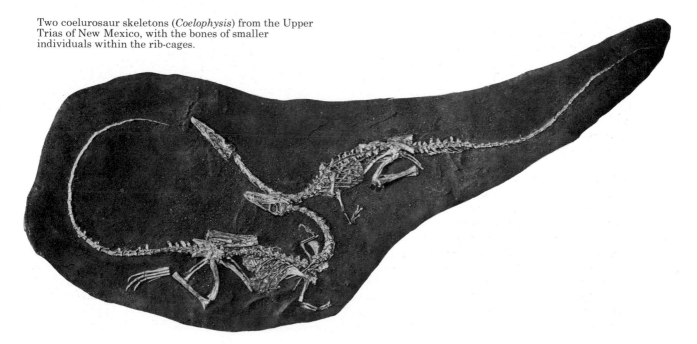

An egg of a primitive horned dinosaur (*Protoceratops*) from the Upper Cretaceous of Mongolia. Length 15.5 centimetres.

Right. Fragments of egg-shell, somewhat enlarged, to show the outer surface. The straight bottom edge of the lowermost fragment measures 13 millimetres.

A coprolite, a fossilized dropping, perhaps from a dinosaur. Length 29 centimetres.

Left The hind footprint of an *Iguanodon*, from the Lower Cretaceous of Dorset. Width of entire footprint 24 centimetres.
Above. Last toe-bone of an *Iguanodon*, grooved to support a horny 'hoof'; it fits the centre toe-impression perfectly. Length 9.5 centimetres.

A greatly enlarged section through a diseased dinosaur limb-bone. It used to be thought that this was a cancer, but it now seems that the abnormality is more like that found in domestic fowls suffering from *avian osteopetrosis*.

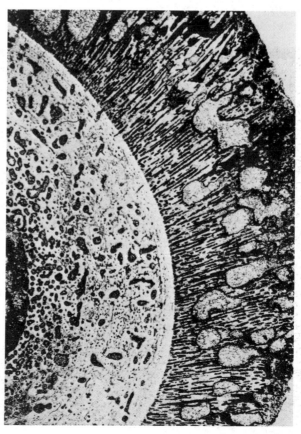

the footprints – unless, in the rocks in question, there seems to be only one sort of dinosaur big enough to be held responsible. Finally, we also know of dinosaur bones which show signs of injury or disease.

So, all in all, we have a great deal of evidence to study – most of it bones and teeth, but a certain amount of other evidence too. In Chapter 8 we shall see how this evidence is used to build up a picture of what the animal looked like when it was still alive, what it ate and how it behaved. There is no other way to acquire this knowledge – until someone invents a time-machine to take us back to the Age of Dinosaurs! But even without a time-machine we can tell – more or less accurately – how long ago each dinosaur lived; the next chapter will explain, very briefly, one method of making such estimates.

Above. The near-parallel trackways of three bipedal dinosaurs, probably *Megalosaurus*, in a Purbeck Stone quarry at Swanage, Dorset. The photograph was taken in 1962.

1 *Right*. Southern Germany in Late Triassic times. A pair of small coelurosaurs (*Procompsognathus*) threaten each other in the foreground. Farther away are two individuals of the great prosauropod *Plateosaurus*.

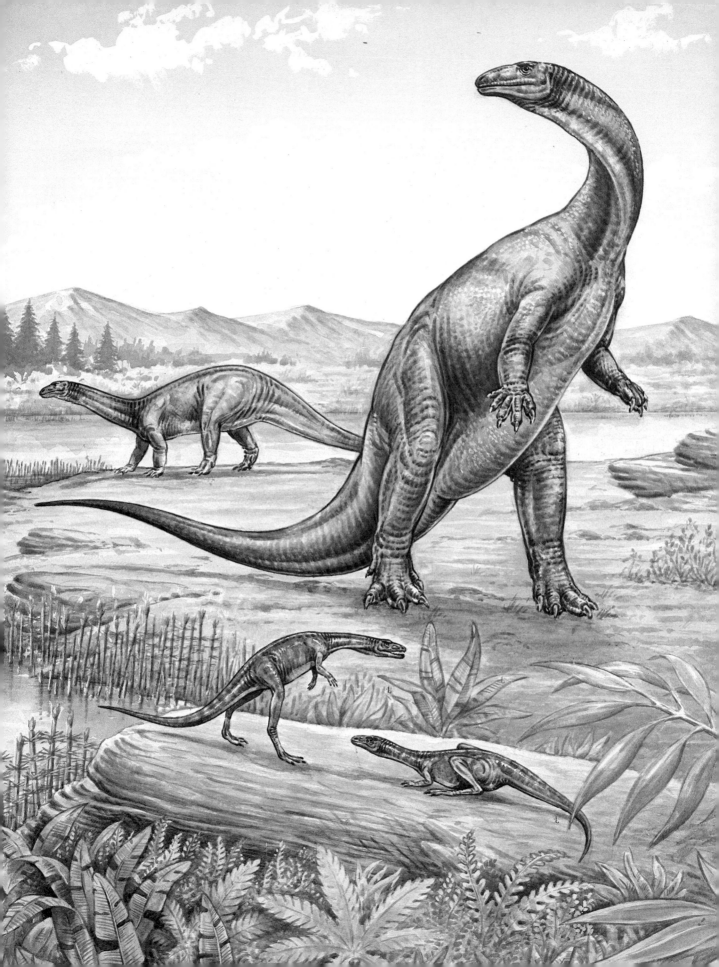

4 · Fossils and time

As we saw in the previous chapter, each layer of sediment deposited at the bottom of the sea (or of a lake, or on land) is likely to contain the remains of animals or plants, or even both, which had been living at that time. Layer was deposited upon layer, sand and silt and mud; but, while this was going on, the animals and plants were slowly changing. Now, millions of years later, the results of this slow evolution are still clearly visible. If we examine a cliff-face which shows several layers of hardened sediment cut through like a cake, we find that the fossilized animals and plants in each layer or *stratum* are different from those in the strata above and below. The farther apart the strata, the more different are the fossils. Each stratum, in fact, contains a set of fossils which are characteristic of the age during which the stratum was laid down. This is just as true of the dinosaurs as of any other living organisms; it will be remembered that at the end of Chapter 1 we said that each period during the Age of Dinosaurs had its own characteristic 'collection' of these remarkable animals.

Many of the fossil species, when alive, were widely distributed across the globe; this is especially true of those that lived in the sea. Others, so it seems, lived only in limited areas; but in other areas with the same sort of environment their place in the scheme of things was filled by their close relatives – just as, today, we have the African elephant in Africa and the Indian elephant in India and south-east Asia.

Sea-cliffs east of Hastings, Sussex. The stratified section is through the Hastings Beds, which are part of the Wealden Formation (i.e. Lower Cretaceous).

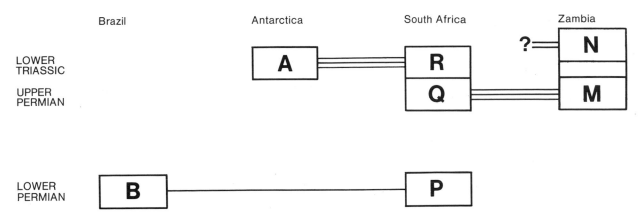

A simple diagram to show how strata in different continents are correlated by means of the fossils which they contain.

Fossils like these, which change with time but not at all (or hardly at all) with distance, are very useful in what we call *relative dating*. For example, because a certain fossil reptile has been found in a certain stratum in South Africa (R in figure above) and the same reptile, or something very like it, in a certain stratum in Antarctica (A), it is probable that the two strata were laid down at about the same time – but we cannot say how long ago. Indeed, on one sort of fossil alone we could well be wrong, it might just happen to have been one of those rare species that survived unaltered for a very long time. However, the presence in the South African stratum of *three* different fossils, each with its counterpart in the Antarctic deposit, makes it almost certain that the two strata are of about the same age.

We then observe that immediately below R in South Africa lies another stratum Q – presumably a little older than R – which contains several fossils linking Q in similar fashion with a stratum M in Zambia (Central Africa). This tells us that the Zambian stratum too is older than the South African stratum R we were discussing in the paragraph above and, moreover, older than the stratum from Antarctica. Lower still in South Africa is a stratum P containing a very characteristic fossil found nowhere else except in the Brazilian stratum B; this shows that B is of the same age as P and older than all the other strata mentioned. And so we continue, working in this manner from one country to another, gradually building up a

scale of comparative ages for the strata. What this *cannot* tell us, however, is the *absolute* ages of the rocks and the fossils – their actual ages in millions of years; we can say only that stratum M is of the same age as Q, older than R, younger than P and so on. In the same way we could say that John is of the same age as Peter, a little older than Andrew and a little younger than George, without having the least idea of whether the persons concerned were all small children or old-age pensioners!

This method can still be used (although less reliably) even when there is no direct correlation between the fossils in two strata. Thus the figure shows also a stratum N in the Zambian succession, lying above M and presumably younger than the latter; it contains fossils which are generally similar to those found in R and A but are not precisely identical or even approximately so. This means that we cannot tell for sure whether N is contemporaneous with R and A, a little older or a little younger; we can, however, express an opinion on that question according to whether the fossils in N – considered all together – are equally, less or more highly evolved than the fossil assemblage found in R and A.

For their own convenience geologists have grouped all the strata into *systems* and given them names. The time during which a system was deposited is called a *period* and is given the same name. Thus the strata of the Silurian system were laid down in what is called the Silurian period; the Silurian system is above the Ordovician system and below the Devonian system, just as the Silurian period is after the Ordovician period and before the Devonian

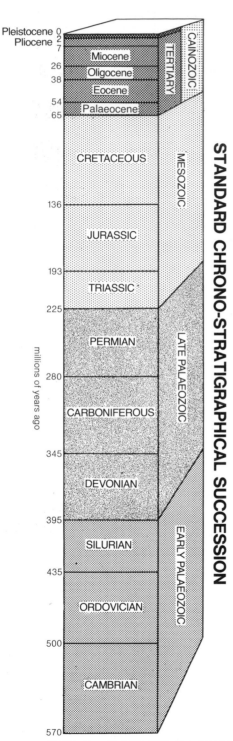

The Holocene or Recent, the 10,000 years which have elapsed since the end of the Pleistocene, is much too short a period to be shown on this scale.

period. All these names are shown in the stratigraphical column (*see* figure). Each system may be subdivided into Lower, Middle and Upper portions; each period may be subdivided correspondingly into Early, Middle and Late.

Although so far we have been talking only of *comparative dating*, there are methods of estimating the real ages of rocks and fossils in thousands and millions of years. The best-known and most up-to-date of these is based upon the decay of radioactive elements, some of which (usually a minute proportion) were included in the rock when it was formed or in the fossil when it was a living animal or plant. *Half* of a radioactive element breaks up in a fixed time characteristic of that element ('half-life') and then half of what is left in the same length of time again, and so on for ever. Thus, if we can measure how far this process of decay has already gone, we can work out how long it is since the rock was formed or the animal or plant was alive. One element of this sort is radioactive carbon or C^{14} (abbreviated to 'radiocarbon') which forms a small fixed proportion of the carbon in all living organisms; the quantity present starts to decrease immediately after death. Radiocarbon, however, decays very quickly, with a half-life of about 5730 years. Indeed, it should not be used to date fossils more than about 40 000 years old at most, because after that the amount of radiocarbon remaining becomes so small that it cannot be measured accurately. As yet we have no radiometric method (that is, one based on radioactivity) for the direct absolute dating of dinosaurs. The best we can do is to measure the age of lava beds lying above or below the dinosaur strata, using a method based on a very much slower radioactive decay (potassium-argon, with a half-life of 1 310 000 000 years). Nevertheless, using our comparative time-scale and putting in absolute dates wherever we can, we are able to get a pretty good idea of the real age of most fossils.

Let us return to the dinosaurs themselves. They have been found only in the rocks of the Upper Triassic and, above them, throughout the whole of the Jurassic and Cretaceous systems (*see* Plate 17). In higher, younger strata there are no more dinosaurs. Therefore the dinosaurs can have lived only in Late Triassic, Jurassic and Cretaceous times (approximately

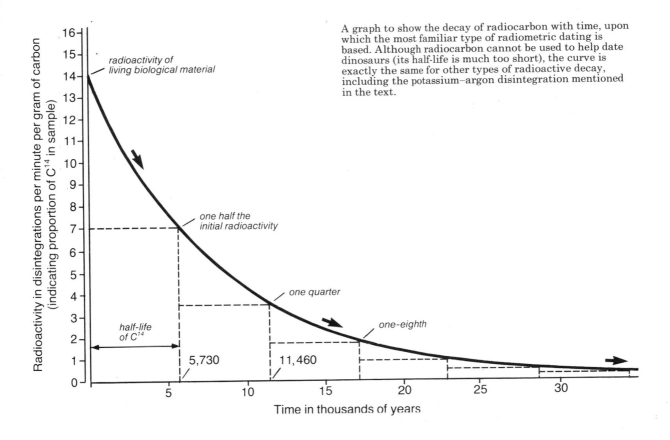

A graph to show the decay of radiocarbon with time, upon which the most familiar type of radiometric dating is based. Although radiocarbon cannot be used to help date dinosaurs (its half-life is much too short), the curve is exactly the same for other types of radioactive decay, including the potassium–argon disintegration mentioned in the text.

205–193, 193–136 and 136–65 million years ago respectively). Since they disappeared the dominant large animals on land have been the mammals, as they still are today. The only reptiles to survive the mysterious mass extinctions at the end of the Cretaceous were all members of the groups that are still with us – turtles and tortoises, lizards and snakes, crocodiles of various sorts, and a strange little lizard-like creature called a tuatara which now lives only on a few small islands off the coast of New Zealand. As might be expected, these last 65 million years are called the Age of Mammals.

Mammals, however, are nothing whatever to do with dinosaurs. They evolved from an entirely different group of extinct reptiles called the mammal-like reptiles, which, although proper reptiles, already possessed some mammal-like characters; the well-known *Cynognathus*, for example, was a great lizard-like creature

A mammal-like reptile, *Cynognathus*, from the Lower Trias of South Africa. Typical length 1.8 metres.

with a thick powerful tail but with a head more like a dog's. Now it might be thought, quite reasonably, that the mammal-like reptiles lived at a time *after* the Age of Reptiles (which is more or less the same thing as the Age of Dinosaurs) and *before* the Age of Mammals. Strangely enough, such a belief could hardly be more wrong. The first mammal-like reptiles were

among the first of all the reptiles and reached their greatest numbers and importance before the dinosaurs had even started their long history. They almost died out as the dinosaurs were beginning – it might even be said that the dinosaurs took over; a few of the mammal-like reptiles survived, however, to become the earliest mammals, living a little later than the first dinosaurs. They were not big like the dinosaurs, not even as big as the mammal-like reptiles from which they had evolved. Indeed, they were tiny

Left. The tuatara (*Sphenodon*) of New Zealand. Typical length 60 centimetres.

A rough guide to the relative fortunes since the Carboniferous of the mammal-like reptiles and their descendants on the one hand, and of the archosaurs and their descendants on the other

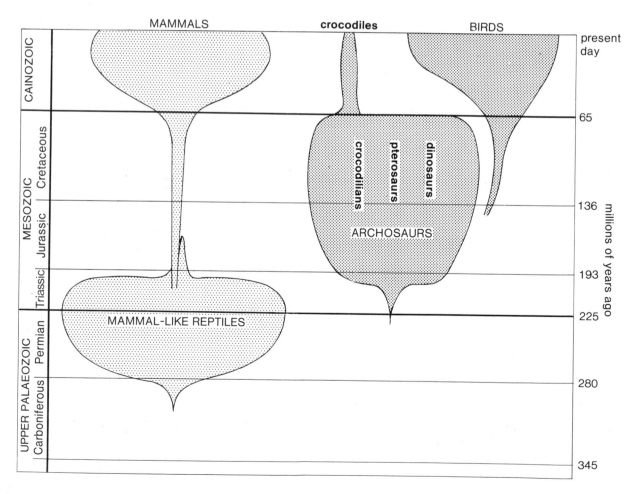

One of the earliest mammals, *Megazostrodon*, from the Lower Jurassic of Basutoland (now Lesotho). Length about 10 centimetres.

creatures, no bigger than the shrews of today; and for the whole of the dinosaurs' 140-million-year reign they lived quietly in the under-growth, in cracks in the rocks and perhaps in burrows, probably terrified of the flesh-eating dinosaurs and daring to come out only at night to catch the insects upon which they fed. For the whole of that time, too, they remained small; even the largest was no bigger than a hedgehog. Only when the dinosaurs had at last died out, at the end of the Cretaceous, did the mammals become dominant, rapidly evolving into a wide variety of different forms and at the same time increasing greatly in size.

The question is sometimes asked whether it is possible that dinosaurs are in fact *not* extinct, whether in some remote part of the world living dinosaurs remain undiscovered. It is a fascinating suggestion, which more than one author has used as the basis for a novel; the most famous, I suppose, is Conan Doyle's *Lost World*. And if it *were* true, how wonderful it would be. It could help us solve many riddles as yet unanswered; for example, were dinosaurs cold-blooded or warm-blooded, what colour were they, what sort of noises did they make? Sad to relate, their continued existence cannot be regarded as even a remote possibility. It is not just the fact that the rocks laid down in the last 65 million years have never yielded as much as one dinosaur bone. There is the equally impressive fact that the land surface of the earth has now been so thoroughly explored (and

surveyed from the air) that a breeding population of gigantic animals could hardly exist without ever being seen by any of the three or four thousand million human inhabitants of the globe – not even by one of them, on just *one* occasion. Admittedly, dinosaurs could have survived unseen in Antarctica, but the frozen wastes of Antarctica would be much too cold for them; likewise they might have lived on in the depths of the oceans, but, as far as we know, no dinosaur ever took to salt water.

By the way, if the last dinosaur really did die 65 million years ago, and if the human race goes back only some 2 million or so, what about all those countless cartoons, stories and films which show dinosaurs and prehistoric man living at the same time? (Prehistoric man is often depicted as a shaggy individual with a low brow and a receding jaw, wearing only an animal skin and armed with a knobbly club, who has just killed a *Brontosaurus* for his dinner.) Alas, such cartoons and films cannot be taken seriously; no human being could ever have tasted brontosaur flesh, or fled in panic from the jaws of a passing *Tyrannosaurus*!

Are you sure their brains are only the size of peas?'

2 *Overleaf*. The western U.S.A. in Late Jurassic times. In the foreground a carnosaur (*Ceratosaurus*) feeds on the carcass of a sauropod (*Apatosaurus*; = *Brontosaurus*). Two small coelurosaurs (*Coelurus*) are joining in the feast. Farther away an even bigger sauropod, the gigantic *Brachiosaurus*, ambles towards the left, while the plated *Stegosaurus* walks in front of it in the opposite direction. Two ornithopods (*Camptosaurus*) are in the background on the left, and another *Apatosaurus* veers away towards the rear.

5 · The evolutionary tree

If we accept the fact of evolution we shall realize that all forms of life, both past and present, may be arranged into a 'family tree'. Here we are particularly concerned with animals. A proper family tree, showing the relationships within a human family, is usually drawn with the oldest generation at the top and the youngest at the bottom. The opposite is true of a family tree of the animal kingdom, in whole or in part (*see* figure P opposite), which is conventionally drawn with time progressing up a vertical scale towards the top. This has two advantages. First, the fossil animals are shown in the same relative positions – oldest at the bottom, youngest at the top – as the geological strata in which they are found. Secondly, the 'tree' is the same way up as a real tree, with a trunk below dividing upwards into branches, even though it is somewhat unusual in that all the branches are growing upwards, either straight up or obliquely, and keeping their growing tips at the same horizontal level – the present time. Those tips, indeed, represent species that are alive today; the tips lower down, which have ceased to grow at various times in the past, represent species that have become extinct without leaving any descendants. As we know, however, not all extinct species have died out completely like this; some have merely been transformed with the passage of time into new species, and, although they themselves were once alive and situated at the growing tips of twigs of the evolutionary tree, those twigs have grown upwards a long way since then and the species concerned now lie far back down the branches.

Any horizontal section through the tree will show a slice of every branch or twig reaching that level, representing every species living at that time, i.e. the whole *fauna* or collection of animals then existing, but it will show nothing else; there will be nothing to show the relationships between the species (except that the closer the slices are to each other the more likely is it that they were closely related), nothing to show that other branches had died off earlier, not even anything to suggest the existence of the evolutionary tree itself. Only by studying a whole series of such sections (each representing a fossil-bearing stratum, or strata, of a certain age) can we gain any knowledge of these matters; and the more sections we can study, the more reference points shall we have and the more accurately shall we be able to fill in the details of the pattern of branching of the tree. This pattern is not just a theoretical idea but an objective reality; living organisms really did evolve in one particular way. But alas, our knowledge of the pattern is woefully incomplete.

In Chapter 2 we discussed what was meant by a species; most helpful was the idea that members of a species usually bred only with each other. This is all very well when we are talking about species of the present day, or indeed of any one particular time, when all the species we know are represented by the separate slices on a single horizontal section through the evolutionary tree. It is not so easy, however, when we are considering the *whole* tree with the extra 'vertical' dimension of time, when everything is continuous with everything else and when species change, more or less gradually, into other species. We cannot test the interbreeding capabilities of animals long dead which, in any case, lived at different times from each other, nor do we know where one species should end and its successor begin; indeed, solutions to problems of this nature can be no more than opinions, never definitive answers. We are greatly hindered also by our complete ignorance of most of the tree. In palaeontology, however, species are defined not by their limits but by what we hope are their centres; each species, when first pub-

The Tree of Life
P. A family tree is growing upwards through time to the present day; all its branches are in continuity. It has been cut through horizontally at three levels, each representing the time of deposition of a stratum from which a good fossil collection has been made.
Q. Without the tree, however, the animals – living and fossil – are represented only by separate spots on the sections A–D, quite different on each section and seemingly unrelated to those on the others.

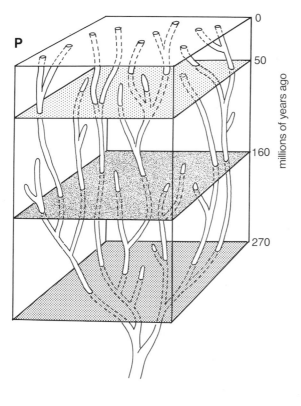

P

millions of years ago

0
50
160
270

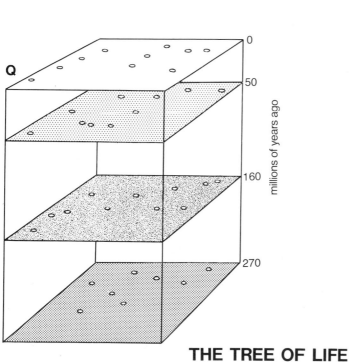

Q

millions of years ago

0
50
160
270

THE TREE OF LIFE

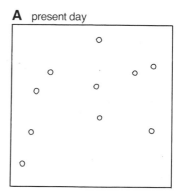

A   present day

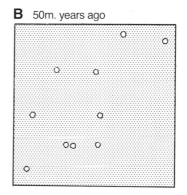

B   50m. years ago

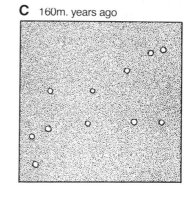

C   160m. years ago

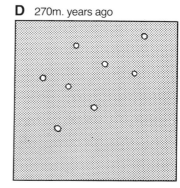

D   270m. years ago

lished, should have been based on one individual specimen as the standard of reference, the 'type' of that species. This means that we can at least try to describe every new specimen we find by reference to an existing type, either placing it positively in the same species if it is closely similar or, when there are slight differences in form or when poor or incomplete preservation makes adequate comparison impossible, assigning it to the species in a more tentative manner. Sometimes, however, we find that the characters of a new specimen suggest that it is intermediate between two other widely separated forms yet is too far from either to be assigned, even tentatively, to one or the other. Alternatively (and more frequently) we may find that the new specimen seems to represent a twig, the existence of which was unsuspected until now, apparently diverging from one of the known branches of the evolutionary tree. In such cases we feel justified in proposing and naming a new species, taking our new specimen as the type.

It is obviously desirable that types should be well-preserved specimens, as complete as possible, situated at suitable intervals in the evolutionary succession. Existing types, however (especially those designated by scientists of previous generations) are often highly unsatisfactory and – short of rejecting the species altogether – there is nothing that we can do about it. Even when choosing our own types for new species we often find that our choice, like Hobson's, is limited by the shortage of material.

Incidentally, when trying to fit a fossil species into the evolutionary tree we must remember that its level has to accord with its relative age – if the latter is known. We cannot fit a Triassic fossil on to a branch that did not originate until the Early Cretaceous! When we do not know the age of the species it is perfectly legitimate to reverse the process, using the characters of the new species to estimate its position in the evolutionary tree and then using that position to determine, with proper caution, the relative age of the fossil and of the rock in which it was found.

This chapter, we hope, has revealed the nature of the palaeontologist's most important task. It is to find out more about the life of bygone ages and then, using that increased knowledge, to acquire a fuller understanding of how plants and animals evolved; in other words, to elucidate their family trees.

6 · First discoveries

Dinosaurs (or the bones of dinosaurs) have been present on this earth for more than 200 million years, but no one had ever heard of them until 1841. There was an excellent reason for this: until 1824, little more than 150 years before this book was written, no one had even realized that such things existed, and it was another seventeen years after that before someone invented a name for them.

A 'human thigh-bone' from Oxfordshire, as figured and described by Plot in 1676. It is actually the lower end of a dinosaur thigh-bone, probably *Megalosaurus*.

Of course, even before 1824 people had been finding strange-looking bones of enormous size buried in the ground, but nobody really knew what they were. It was thought by some that they were the bones of giant men! The earliest book to mention such a bone was published by the Reverend Robert Plot of Oxford in 1676, and more of these bones were found in the eighteenth century. But the story of dinosaurs really began in 1822, the year when the first teeth of *Iguanodon* were discovered. Those same teeth are still to be seen in London, in the palaeontological collections of the Natural History Museum.

The first important character in our story is Gideon Mantell (1790–1852), a young country doctor who lived and worked in the little Sussex town of Lewes. It so happened that he was also a very keen collector of fossils, mostly from the South Downs, and wrote books and articles on the subject. One sunny spring day in 1822 he had

Rev. Dr Robert Plot (1640–1696)

driven into the surrounding countryside to visit a patient, and, because the day was so beautiful, his wife Mary Ann had decided to accompany him. While Dr Mantell was indoors with his patient, Mrs Mantell took a stroll along the lane and made a scientific discovery of the greatest importance. For there, in a pile of stones from the local quarry, soon to be used for repairs to the road surface, was something dark brown and shiny. Closer examination showed that one of the pieces of sandstone contained

Gideon Algernon Mantell (1790–1852)

Mary Ann Woodhouse, Mrs Mantell

Some of the original *Iguanodon* teeth found by Dr and Mrs Mantell. The tooth on the right is 5.3 centimetres long as preserved.

large fossil teeth quite unlike anything that Mrs Mantell (or seemingly anyone else) had ever seen before.

Mrs Mantell showed the teeth to her husband. He became very excited; he managed to find out which quarry the teeth had come from, near Cuckfield in Sussex, but the rest of the animal was never found. However, more teeth and large bones were found in the quarry and in others nearby. What really excited Mantell was this. The teeth were suitable for slicing up tough vegetable matter, like those of some mammals of the present day, and had probably belonged to a gigantic plant-eater; but they were found in rocks of Cretaceous age, too old (as was then thought) to contain any mammals. This met with flat disbelief from the famous scientists of the time – among them the celebrated naturalist Baron Georges Cuvier of Paris (1769–1832), generally regarded as the founder of the study of comparative anatomy. They all thought that the teeth *were* mammal teeth, and that Mantell was mistaken in think-

ing that they came from Cretaceous rocks; they must have come (so said the scientists) from overlying rocks deposited much later.

Mantell, however, knew that he was not mistaken. He discovered that his fossil teeth were like those of an iguana lizard from Central America, and he decided to call the unknown animal from which they came *Iguanodon* – 'iguana-tooth'. He published a description of the teeth and bones of *Iguanodon* in 1825. We now know that in many things Mantell was wrong. He pictured the animal as a proper

The Common Iguana of Central and South America. Typical length 1.2 metres.

A quarry in the Tilgate Forest, Sussex, with the spire of Cuckfield Parish Church in the background. From a lithograph in Mantell's 'Geology of Sussex' (1827).

quadruped, walking on all four legs, but much better skeletons found more than fifty years later (*see* below) show that it often walked on its back legs alone (*see* also Plates 4 and 5). Mantell also made an amusing error in taking the animal's spiky thumb-bone (of which he had found only one) and placing it on top of its snout as though the creature were a rhinoceros! But these mistakes do not matter much. The really important thing that Mantell did, in which he was quite right, was to recognize that in the long distant past, before mammals ruled the earth, there had existed gigantic reptiles – far bigger than any known today – of which at least some fed on plants. Mantell's belief was endorsed by Cuvier, who, informed of the new evidence in 1824 (before it was published), had very sensibly accepted Mantell's identification of the material as reptilian and admitted that he himself had been mistaken in thinking that it came from a mammal.

3 *Left*. Southern England in Early Jurassic times. The carnosaur *Megalosaurus* catches sight of a possible victim, the primitive ornithischian *Scelidosaurus*.

A model of Waterhouse Hawkins' restoration of *Iguanodon*

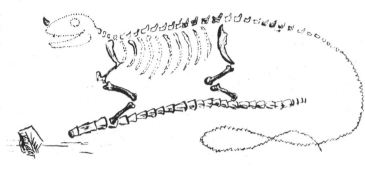

Iguanodon, as restored by Mantell. The horn on the animal's nose is actually one of its thumbs. From Mantell's original drawing in the British Museum (Natural History).

The lower end of the right shin-bone of an *Iguanodon* from Cuckfield, obtained by William Smith in 1809. Length of fragment 38 centimetres.

It is of interest to note that, since this chapter was first drafted, we have discovered in the collections of the Natural History Museum in London an *Iguanodon* bone which, so it would appear, was collected at Cuckfield in 1809 – thirteen years before Mrs Mantell's famous discovery. It was obtained by William Smith, 'Father of English Geology', who, of course, had no idea at all of what it was that he had acquired. It has also been claimed that Dean Buckland of Oxford University had found *Iguanodon* bones in the Isle of Wight a few years before the Mantells' discoveries in Sussex.

Meanwhile other discoveries were taking place. Several bones of another enormous reptile, as big as *Iguanodon* but with teeth suitable for eating meat, had been dug up at Stonesfield in Oxfordshire even before Mrs Mantell's discovery of 1822, for Cuvier saw it in Oxford as early as 1818. The animal was named *Megalosaurus* ('big lizard'; *see* also Plate 3) and a description of it was published by Buckland in 1824. (Perhaps *Megalosaurus*, rather than *Iguanodon*, really deserves to be called the first dinosaur, for its skeleton was not only the first to be found but also the first to be properly named. Unfortunately Buckland, although a professional geologist, did not recognize its importance.) In 1832 Mantell described another very different reptile skeleton from Sussex (*Hylaeosaurus*), and in 1834 he obtained a whole mass of *Iguanodon* bones – with teeth as well – from a quarry in Maidstone, Kent. (The latter discovery became so famous that, in 1949, the Borough of Maidstone was permitted to incorporate an *Iguanodon* in its coat of arms as a

Richard – later Sir Richard – Owen (1804–1892)

The Maidstone *Iguanodon*, from Bensted's quarry. Width
as preserved exactly 2 metres.

supporter.) Throughout the 1830s more giant
reptiles were discovered, abroad as well as in
England, and by 1841 nine different sorts were
known – some, it must be admitted, from rather
scrappy remains.

Then, in 1841, at a meeting in Plymouth of the
British Association for the Advancement of
Science, Dr Richard Owen (1804–1892; later
Professor Sir Richard Owen, first Director of
the Natural History Museum in South Kensington) suggested that *Iguanodon*, *Megalosaurus*
and *Hylaeosaurus* should together be called the
Dinosauria, the 'terrible lizards'. (A fourth
British dinosaur, *Cetiosaurus*, was already
known at the time, but Owen thought it was a
crocodile.) The dinosaurs could be recognized
by their gigantic size and by certain peculiarities unknown in other reptiles.

The *Iguanodon* skeletons from Bernissart, displayed in the
Royal National Institute of Natural Sciences in Brussels.

Members of the general public soon came to
hear of these newly discovered monsters of the
prehistoric world. Indeed, their interest was
deliberately fostered by the construction in
South London, in the grounds of the Crystal
Palace at Sydenham, of several life-sized restorations of extinct amphibians, reptiles (including all of Owen's dinosaurs) and mammals.
They were built of cement, stone, bricks, tiles
and iron by the sculptor Waterhouse Hawkins,
working under Owen's direction, and they were
completed in 1854. A particularly memorable
event took place on New Year's Eve, 1853, when
Hawkins and Owen held a dinner party – at the
unusual hour of four o'clock in the afternoon –
for twenty distinguished guests, about a dozen
of the party being seated *inside* the partially
completed model of the *Iguanodon*. Despite the
fact that all the dinosaur restorations are, in
the light of modern knowledge, utterly and
completely wrong (both *Iguanodon* and *Megalosaurus* having been restored as quadrupeds),
the exhibit proved immensely popular; and,

despite the burning down of the Crystal Palace
in 1936, the concrete animals remain there to
this day in the good care of the Greater London
Council.

Thus it was that the idea of dinosaurs was
born and began to be known more widely. As it
happened, not many more really exciting dinosaur discoveries were to be made in Britain;
North America was the scene of most of the
action during the second half of the nineteenth
century. But before we cross the Atlantic we
must mention the remarkable find made in a
coal-mine in the Belgian town of Bernissart in
1877 and 1878. More than 300 metres below the
surface the miners found themselves tunnelling
through a mass of what turned out to be
Iguanodon skeletons. It took three years to

4 *Right. Iguanodon* in concrete, as conceived by Owen
and restored by Waterhouse Hawkins; in the grounds of
the Crystal Palace, South London

A twentieth-century restoration of *Iguanodon*, by Vernon Edwards

excavate them from the mine. In the Royal National Institute of Natural Sciences in Brussels there are now thirty-one of these dinosaurs; eleven complete skeletons are properly mounted in a standing position, and twenty more, complete or incomplete, are exhibited lying down. It was these specimens which showed up the errors in Mantell's and Owen's reconstructions of *Iguanodon*.

Just when the Belgian dinosaurs were being excavated the first important discoveries were being made in the American West, mostly in the states of Colorado, Utah, Wyoming, Montana and (later) New Mexico. This part of the world was still being opened up, and the collectors were often in danger of attack by Indians. The most famous area is around the little town of Medicine Bow in Wyoming, familiar to everyone who has followed the tale of *The Virginian*. There the ground was littered for miles with the bones of gigantic dinosaurs, well preserved and easy to collect. Indeed, in one place there were

so many bones that a shepherd had built himself a little cabin out of them. It was possible to collect nearly complete skeletons in enormous numbers, as is shown by the well-stocked Dinosaur Halls of so many major American museums. An amusing side to this story lies in the fierce hatred for each other of two rival professors, Edward Drinker Cope (1840–1897) and Othniel Charles Marsh (1831–1899), each of whom tried to collect and name more new dinosaurs than the other. When they started only nine dinosaurs had been named from the whole of North America, but by the time they had finished they had, between them, named 136 more!

New discoveries have come thick and fast in the earlier part of the present century. Another famous dinosaur site in the United States is near the town of Vernal, in Utah. Discovered in 1909, the strata (packed with enormous dinosaur bones) have been tilted by earth movements so that they are now almost vertical, with

A technician working on the cliff face at Dinosaur
National Monument, Utah

Street sign in Dinosaur, Colorado

their top surface forming the face of a cliff 9
metres high and nearly 60 metres long. This cliff
has been incorporated into a special building, a
unique museum, in which visitors can walk
along a lower gallery or an upper gallery and
watch the skilled technicians exposing the
bones on the cliff face. The whole area around
the site is called Dinosaur National Monument;
its official headquarters are just across the state
boundary in Colorado, outside a little town
once called Artesia but now renamed Dinosaur.
Even the streets in Dinosaur have names like
Brontosaurus Boulevard, Stegosaurus Freeway
or Triceratops Terrace.

5 *Overleaf*. South-eastern England in Early Cretaceous
times. Two small ornithopods (*Hypsilophodon*) browse in
the right foreground, while the armoured *Polacanthus*
walks behind them. On the left of the picture are two
much bigger ornithopods, the famous *Iguanodon*. The
only meat-eater represented here is the little-known
carnosaur *Altispinax*, seen in the distance.

Above. The shoulder-blade of a gigantic sauropod, excavated at Tendaguru in German East Africa (now Tanzania) in the early years of this century

Left. Dinosaurs in the Sahara: a backbone of *Ouranosaurus*, exposed by the action of wind, in north-eastern Niger

Other countries where dinosaurs were found abundantly before World War I were Canada (in the valley of the Red Deer River, Alberta) and German East Africa – now Tanzania. Since World War I more new dinosaur deposits have been discovered; the richest of these is in the Gobi Desert of Mongolia, but other promising areas are China, India, the Sahara and Argentina. The only continent that, as yet, has yielded no remains of these great reptiles is Antarctica; and palaeontologists have little doubt that even there, beneath the ice, dinosaur bones await discovery – reminders of the warm Antarctic climate of the distant long ago.

7 · Hunting for dinosaurs

We should all like to find buried treasure in the garden – perhaps a hoard of Roman coins, in silver and gold, or mediaeval ornaments encrusted with precious stones. No matter where we live, there is always the possibility, the very faint hope that we might be lucky, for buried treasure could be discovered anywhere. It would also be exciting to find a dinosaur. But here we must be more careful, for, if we think about it, there are only certain places where it is even *possible* for a dinosaur to be found.

Dinosaurs, like all fossils, can be found only in rocks formed from the sediments in which their remains were buried, sediments like mud and sand. We have seen in Chapter 3 how those sediments are changed into sedimentary rocks like clay and sandstone. By contrast, rocks formed directly from the molten interior of the earth (*igneous* rocks like granite and basalt) never contain fossils of any sort – except, very rarely, for impressions on the surface of lava flows. It must also be remembered that dinosaurs lived only in Late Triassic, Jurassic and Cretaceous times – from about 205 million years ago to 65 million years ago; this means that we cannot expect to find their bones in any sedimentary rocks below the Upper Trias or above the top of the Cretaceous. And dinosaurs were land animals; so, as a general rule, we cannot hope to discover their remains in sediments that were laid down at the bottom of the sea (as most sediments are).

Sometimes, however, dinosaur skeletons *are* found in sea-floor deposits, for the corpses of land animals do occasionally float down a river and out into the ocean. In England, for example, the Oxford Clay of Bedfordshire and Cambridgeshire – laid down at the bottom of the Late Jurassic sea – is dug for making bricks; and, while most of the fossil reptile skeletons found in the claypits are those of sea-creatures (like ichthyosaurs and plesiosaurs), dinosaur skeletons too turn up from time to time. But this happens so rarely that, in practice, it is a waste of time to go deliberately looking for dinosaurs in salt-water deposits.

Where we should really hunt is in freshwater deposits, laid down in swamps, lakes or rivers, maybe in deltas; we might also find what we are looking for in deposits laid down on dry land (volcanic ash and dune sands). The best area for dinosaurs in England is in the Wealden rocks (Lower Cretaceous) of Sussex and the Isle of Wight, laid down some 120 million years ago in a great subsiding trough which was spasmodically open to the sea. But even there it is now very difficult to find good 'exposures', because the Sussex quarries in which Mantell found his *Iguanodon* bones in the first half of the nineteenth century are no longer worked; they were either filled in, 100 years ago or more, or are now so covered in soil, vegetation and trees that it is impossible to get at the fresh unweathered rock. The dinosaur remains of the Isle of Wight are sometimes almost complete skeletons, with the bones still lying next to each other as they were when joined together in life, but the remains from Sussex are nearly always just scattered bones and teeth or maybe a row of vertebrae from the tail.

Thus it would seem that England is not a very good place in which to hunt for dinosaurs – even though, for its size, it probably has more different sorts of dinosaurs than occur in any other country in the world. Wales, Scotland and Ireland have no dinosaurs at all (except for a few footprints in South Wales). They are, however, especially abundant in certain regions of North America, both Canada and the U.S.A., and they may also be found in quantity in other, less easily accessible parts of the globe. Again, we can expect to find dinosaurs only in land or freshwater deposits of Late Triassic to Late Cretaceous age; and again, there is not much point in making a deliberate search for them except in those areas where they have already been found accidentally.

The question now arises … who would be likely to find a dinosaur bone by accident? It might be a shepherd boy on a hillside. It might be a geologist or an ordinary explorer, making his way on foot through a little-known part of

the world far from civilization (like the western United States 100 years ago, or the Sahara Desert today). Or – as we saw in Chapter 3 – it might be a quarryman or a miner, a civil engineer constructing a new motorway or a labourer digging out for the foundations of a building.

Once we know that dinosaurs have been discovered in a particular area we can be fairly certain that there are more to be found. But we cannot just go out and hunt them. If we want to hunt living animals we have to get permission from the owner of the land we wish to hunt over; we may also need a hunting licence; and if the animal is rare – what is now called an 'endangered species' – we may not be allowed to hunt it at all. It is the same with fossils. In most cases we require permission from the land-owner or the mining company, and in most countries overseas a Government permit is needed to collect vertebrate fossils and to take them abroad. Indeed, such permission is usually given only if the collector agrees that, when he has finished his scientific studies of the fossils, he will return them – or at least some of them – to the country from which they came.

A *Hypsilophodon* skeleton from the Lower Cretaceous of the Isle of Wight, still embedded in the rock. The hip-bones are in the centre, the tail to the left, the backbone to the right, a thigh-bone beneath the tail and ribs on the far right. Total length of specimen as preserved 60.5 centimetres.

Another point is that hunting dinosaurs – like hunting lions or elephant – can be danger-ous. Not, of course, for the same reason; it is simply that the best places for fossil-hunting are in fresh exposures of rock, which means those places where the rock is always crumbling or falling away. And, where the rock has fallen once, it could always fall again.

At long last, however, we can begin our hunt. The area must be searched very patiently; sometimes we may walk and walk and find nothing for days. We need to be very observant for, just as the presence of a fox or a deer is betrayed by its droppings or its footprints (or, to a dog, by its scent), so the presence of a dinosaur skeleton may be shown by a mere scrap of bone on the ground. Much more of the skeleton may lie beneath the ground, or it may be weathering out of the mountain high above and falling down the hillside, piece by piece. Indeed, most of

6 A member of a Polish–Mongolian expedition to the Gobi Desert working on the skeleton of a duck-billed dinosaur

Excavating in Basutoland (now Lesotho)

our finds will consist of no more than scraps of limb-bones, odd vertebrae, loose teeth, or weathered lumps of rock with broken bone showing on the surface. It takes an expert to recognize them for what they are (and they may not be dinosaur at all – they could, for example, have belonged to a crocodile). Where many such pieces are found in one place there may be two animals, or even more, all jumbled up together.

Before we try to collect our fossil we must first make a careful note of its exact position, perhaps taking photographs or making sketches. How we collect it depends a great deal upon the sort of fossil it is. If it is fairly free of the rock which once surrounded it and if it is strong enough, then all there is to do is to pick it up, paint a number on it, wrap it up and pack it. A small tooth may be wrapped in tissue paper and packed in cotton wool in a matchbox; a great thigh-bone a metre long may be wrapped in

Plastering a skull in Northern Rhodesia (now Zambia)

sacking and packed in straw in a crate; a hotch-potch of broken bits may be dropped straight into a sample-bag. But it is seldom as simple as that. The skeleton may still be embedded in rock – perhaps a soft clay, or a hard limestone – and it must somehow be extracted from it. It is unnecessary to remove all the rock from the bones at this stage, but obviously we prefer not to carry too much of it. For this task we need a wide variety of tools, ranging from picks and shovels and pneumatic drills, through trowels, old dinner-knives and hammers and chisels to penknives, mounted needles and the tiniest of brushes. Loose fragments are glued back into place, and parts which are too soft and breakable are hardened by means of a special resin solution which is sprayed or painted on.

Very often it is necessary to encase the whole fossil in a block (or several blocks) of plaster of Paris, just as a doctor encases a limb in plaster

Cutting open a plaster jacket in the Palaeontological Laboratory at South Kensington

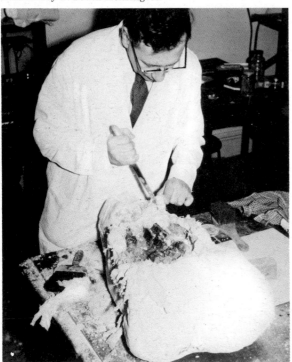

Using an electrically powered engraving tool to clean up a small skull

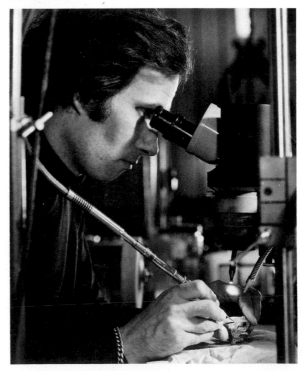

when it has been broken in an accident. A more modern method, however, uses polyurethane foam instead of plaster. The dinosaur is put into these blocks in order to protect the fragile skeleton on its long journey back to the laboratory and to keep all the bones in the same relative positions.

Back in the laboratory there is still a great deal to be done. Some of the broken pieces dropped into the sample-bag, if broken fairly recently and not too badly weathered, may fit together to make larger pieces or even whole bones. Trying to match them up is a fascinating exercise, rather like attempting to solve a three-dimensional jigsaw puzzle with many of the pieces missing and perhaps with pieces of other puzzles mixed in with it. And, with no picture of the finished product, the task is far from easy.

The plaster or polyurethane blocks have to be opened and the softer specimens hardened fur-

ther. All the specimens are now ready for 'development', which means the removal of the rock from around the bones (there is often an especially hard layer of rock immediately next to the bone surface). This can be done in various ways. The oldest way is by hand, using tools ranging from hammer and chisel to a mounted needle so fine that, under the microscope, a skilled technician can pick off one grain of sand at a time. A more modern technique uses electrically powered tools, mostly of the type used by the dentist for drilling holes in teeth. A third method is a sort of sand-blasting with a special machine. The fourth and last method is the chemical method; the specimen is treated with a weak acid which dissolves away the matrix (i.e., the containing rock) but leaves the specimen unharmed. This chemical method gives the finest results, but it works only on certain sorts of matrix and is rather slow.

Using an air-abrasive machine. The machine itself is on the right of the photograph; it produces a blast of gas and abrasive powder through the nozzle of the small tool in the operator's hand. The actual work is carried out in a glass-topped box because it makes so much dust. A convenient source of gas is a cylinder of liquid carbon dioxide.

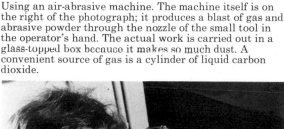

Painting a hardening solution on to the bones of *Scelidosaurus*, exposed by the action of dilute acetic acid on the surrounding rock. The limestone block containing the bones has been partly encased in a protective jacket to support the block and to limit the action of the acid to its upper surface; the jacket is made of plastic reinforced with glass-fibre.

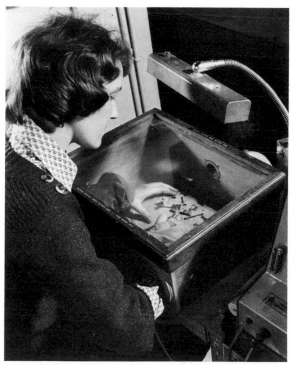

7 A water-colour sketch by Arthur Lakes, an Oxford graduate who worked for Marsh, of a fossil locality in Wyoming; probably painted around 1880 (*see* p.54)

Right. Mounting a *Hypsilophodon* skeleton on a metal framework

Making a glass-fibre cast of part of the hand of an *Iguanodon*. The mould (negative) has already been made and the internal walls of its cavity are being painted with polyester resin.

Eventually, then, we shall become the proud possessors of a fine collection of cleaned and mended dinosaur bones, all (we hope) from the same individual. But there will doubtless be several bones missing, and, even of those bones that *are* represented, many will be far from complete. Thus, if the specimen is required for public exhibition, the missing bones and parts of bones will have to be modelled as realistically as possible. (Until a few years ago such substitutes were made of plaster, but now they are usually made of the much lighter and less breakable – but more expensive – glass-fibre and resin.) The final operation will be when all the bones, real and artificial alike, are mounted on a metal or glass-fibre framework of such a shape that the whole dinosaur appears to stand in a life-like position. A bare skeleton, devoid of flesh; yet – as we shall see in the next chapter – it may serve a far worthier purpose than exciting our curiosity, our amazement, our awe and our wonder. A little simple detective work, a little common sense can often turn a mere collection of old bones like this into a treasure-house of useful information on the prehistoric world.

8 · Dinosaurs as living animals

Mounted dinosaur skeletons are very useful objects for filling museum galleries – partly because they take up a great deal of room, partly because they attract vast numbers of people who come to marvel at their gigantic size and strange appearance. But how many of those people, standing in wonder before a *Diplodocus* or a *Tyrannosaurus rex*, ever stop to ask themselves what the animal looked like when it was alive, what it fed on, how it behaved, and what sort of world it lived in?

It so happens that we can often find the answers to these questions by making a careful study of the dinosaur bones, perhaps comparing them with the bones of living animals, for almost every feature of the shape of each bone and of the structure of the whole skeleton has some significance. A study of non-bony dinosaur fossils (such as footprints) can also prove rewarding. We may even learn a great deal from a list of the other fossils, animal and plant, found with the dinosaurs in the same sediments, and a scientific examination of the sediments themselves can often tell us something of the conditions in which the dinosaurs lived and died. The best way in which we can explain this is by giving some examples of the sort of thing we mean.

First we shall try to reconstruct the shape of the living animal, with the flesh put back on the bones. Most of the flesh (or 'meat') is in fact muscle. A muscle generally runs from one bone to another, being attached to the bone at either end by a fibrous *tendon*; the attachment is marked by a lump or a scar or a slight hollow, all of which can often be seen just as clearly on a fossil bone as on the bone of a freshly killed animal. Now the pattern of muscles in closely related animals is, as a rule, very similar; we can tell from the lumps and scars and hollows on the bones of dinosaurs that their muscle pattern was not too different from the patterns found in their closest living relatives, the crocodiles and the birds. So, if we are able to see the position and the size of the muscle attachments on our dinosaur skeleton, and if we possess a good knowledge of the muscles of crocodiles and birds, we should be able to make an intelligent guess as to the position, shape and size of the dinosaur's muscles. If we are also good at modelling and have an accurate scale model of the dinosaur's skeleton, we should be able to build up its muscles in clay and make a reasonable restoration of the shape of the living animal.

Such a restored model can be used to estimate the dinosaur's weight. First we must ascertain the volume of the model, immersing it completely in water in a measuring tank and noting by how much the water-level rises (the model must not be able to absorb water!). Secondly, we

Measuring the volume of a dinosaur model by displacing water from a full container, to be measured later in the graduated cylinder. This is a slight variation of the method described in the text.

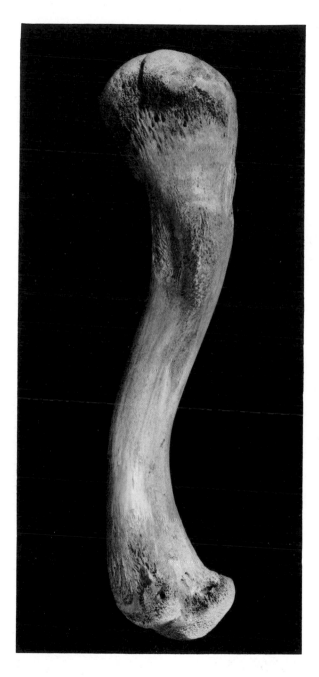 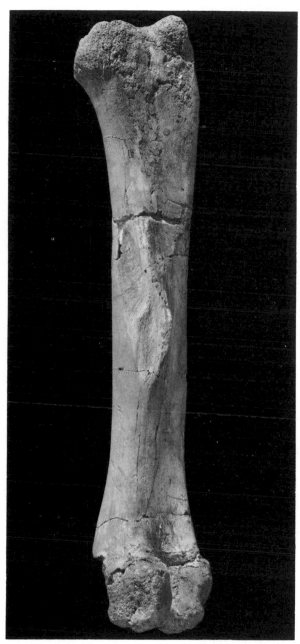

The thigh-bone of a modern crocodile, showing
projections, scars and other areas of muscle attachment.
Length 23 centimetres.

The thigh-bone of a duck-billed dinosaur, *Orthomerus*,
showing the same. Length 49 centimetres.

Putting the finishing touches to a restoration of a sauropod dinosaur (*Apatosaurus*) which has been built up in clay around a wire framework.

Diagrams of the skeleton and of the reconstructed muscles are on the wall behind.

must work out the volume of the actual dinosaur, multiplying the volume of the model by the cube of the scale (for example, if the model is to a scale of one-twentieth we must multiply its volume by $20 \times 20 \times 20$, i.e. 8000). Thirdly, most living reptiles are about 0.9 times as heavy as their own volume of water, so we must multiply the volume of the dinosaur (in millilitres) by 0.9. This will give the dinosaur's weight in grammes.

As mentioned elsewhere, we sometimes find impressions of dinosaur skin – good enough to show its scaly texture, and the absence of feathers or hair. The only thing of which we cannot find evidence is the *colour* of the skin; this we can merely guess at, but if dinosaurs are to be regarded as reptiles we may presume that they could have been as brightly coloured as some of the reptiles of today.

Having completed our picture of the dinosaur itself, we are next faced with the problem: where did it live, on land or in the water? We must choose the right background for our painting! This is sometimes a difficult question to decide, as in the case of the sauropod dinosaurs, *Diplodocus* and its relatives (discussed in some detail in Chapter 13) and that of the duck-billed dinosaurs (Chapter 14).

One of the most important questions with regard to any dinosaur is: was it a quadruped, or a biped, or could it change from two legs to four whenever it wished? It has often been said that the animal must have been a biped if the fore-limbs were much shorter than the hind. This is obviously true in the case of *Tyrannosaurus*, where the fore-limbs are much too small to be of any use in walking; but in *Stegosaurus*, where the fore-limbs are less than half as long as the hind, it is just as obvious (for other reasons) that the animal nevertheless walked quadrupedally at all times. If the front feet are specialized for grasping, then the animal could not have used them for walking and must have been a biped; the same is true if the hind feet *but not the front feet* are specialized for running. On the other hand, hooves on the front feet instead of pointed claws must mean that the dinosaur was quadrupedal for at least some of the time. Fossil footprints can be a big help here, provided that we know which animal made them. If there are impressions of the front feet as well as of the

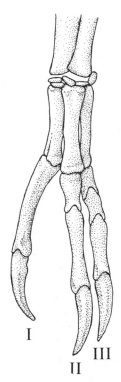

Above. The grasping hand of an ostrich dinosaur, *Ornithomimus*; this hand could not have been used for walking

The hand of an *Iguanodon* to show how some of the terminal toe-bones, judged by their shape, bore horny 'hooves' rather than claws. Width from tip of first digit to tip of fifth digit 39 centimetres.

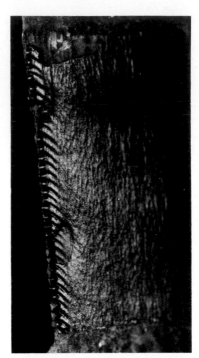

An enlargement of the indicated portion of the serrated edge of the tooth on the left.

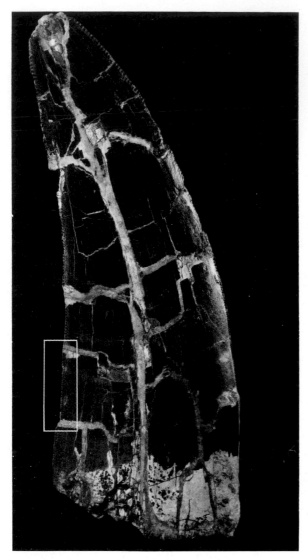

The tooth of a carnosaur (possibly *Megalosaurus*) from the Upper Jurassic of Tanzania. Length 16 centimetres.

Upper cheek teeth of the ornithopod *Heterodontosaurus*, from the Lower Jurassic of southern Africa. Combined span of the seven teeth shown 2.1 centimetres.

hind feet, then the animal was walking on all fours; if there are only hind-foot impressions, then it was walking bipedally. (There is a trackway known with only front-foot impressions. No, the dinosaur was not walking on its hands! It was floating in the water and using its front feet to push on the bottom.)

It should not be too difficult to tell whether or not the dinosaur was able to run quickly. Lightly built animals with long slender legs,

often walking on tiptoe (like modern hoofed mammals) could obviously move more rapidly than great bulky creatures with shorter legs or with thick legs like pillars. It also seems unlikely that dinosaurs that protected themselves with heavy armour (as described in Chapter 15) were capable of any great speed; in any case, speed was less important to them than to their unprotected cousins.

Next we come to the very interesting question

The tooth of a sauropod (possibly *Cetiosauriscus*) from the Upper Jurassic of Cambridgeshire. Length 5.5 centimetres.

Fossil 'mummy' of the duckbill *Anatosaurus*

of the dinosaur's diet. Here, as might be expected, the form of the teeth is highly significant. Some dinosaurs had sharp pointed teeth, curved slightly backwards (*see* figure on far left); the front and back edges are regularly notched, just like a saw or a steak-knife. These were the meat-eaters, using their teeth only to catch their prey and, if it was too big, to slice it into pieces more convenient to swallow. Other dinosaurs had simple teeth, shaped like a peg (*see* figure left), a pencil, a spoon or a leaf; they probably lived on soft vegetation, nipping it off and raking it in. Yet others had much more complicated teeth, ridged and grooved on their inner and outer surfaces, placed close together in one (*see* figure lower left) or several (*see* figures on p.119) rows and worn down by the teeth in the opposite jaw to produce one flat biting surface. Upper and lower teeth together worked like a pair of shears, cutting up the harsh vegetation on which these dinosaurs fed. Finally, a few dinosaurs had no teeth at all; it is generally believed that they lived on small animals, insects, eggs and fruit.

Very rarely (as in the case of the mummified duck-billed dinosaur mentioned in Chapter 14) we can find out exactly what the animal had been eating by a direct examination of the fossilized stomach contents.

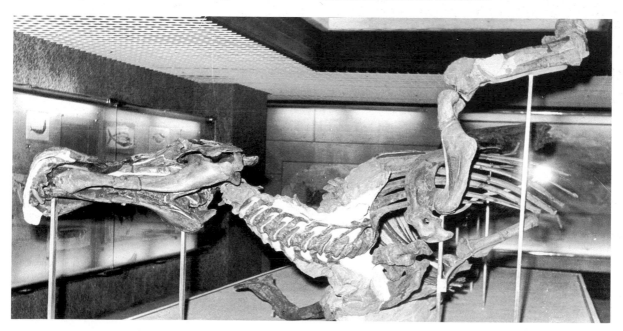

8 The crested duckbill *Corythosaurus* (Late Cretaceous, from western North America)

9 The primitive horned dinosaur *Protoceratops* (Late Cretaceous, from Mongolia)

10 *Pachyrhinosaurus*, the horned dinosaur without a horn (Late Cretaceous, from Alberta)

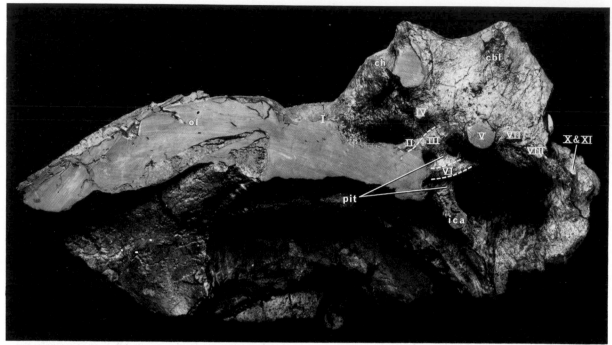

The partial skull of an *Iguanodon*, from the Lower Cretaceous of Sussex, sectioned longitudinally to the left of the midline and with much of the bone removed so that the natural cast of the brain cavity is exposed. The front end is to the left. Length as preserved 41 centimetres. The main part of the brain is top right, the left olfactory lobe is visible in section (light grey) and the roots of the cranial nerves II–VIII on the left side have likewise been cut through. Nerves X and XI of the *right* side are also visible.

ch cerebral hemispheres; cbl cerebellum; ica internal carotid artery; ol olfactory lobe; pit pituitary body; I–XI cranial nerves (II is the optic, VIII the auditory).

The other side of this specimen shows a natural cast of the membranous labyrinth of the inner ear (illustrated in figure on p.29).

At this very moment palaeontologists are arguing fiercely among themselves as to whether dinosaurs were cold-blooded, like modern reptiles, or warm-blooded like mammals and birds. There is a great deal of evidence of many different sorts on this matter, but unfortunately not all of it points in the same direction. Some account of this problem is given in Chapter 16.

Information concerning the animal can also be obtained from its endocranial cast – a cast, natural or artificial, of the cavity of the braincase. During the dinosaur's lifetime the brain fitted fairly closely into the braincase, so that a cast of the cavity provides an almost exact copy of the shape of the brain. The relative sizes of the various parts of the brain tell us, among other things, which senses were the best developed; thus, for example, enlarged optic lobes suggest that vision played an important role in the animal's life.

Many other clues can be found to the dinosaurs' way of life. How did they produce their young? Some of them certainly laid eggs (*see* Chapters 13 and 15); while others, less certainly, may have borne their young alive (Chapter 12). How did they grow? Again, in Chapter 15 we shall see how we are sometimes lucky enough to find individuals of one dinosaur species at every stage of development, from egg to adult. Did they live a solitary life, or did they live in herds? A series of trackways of the same sort of dinosaur, apparently all made at the same time, tells us that that particular species lived gregariously. How did they defend themselves when attacked? This too is very clear from the shape of the armour and of the weapons (such as clubbed or spiked tails) with which Nature sometimes provided them (Chapter 15). Their skeletons occasionally bear the scars of healed wounds (showing that they fought among them-

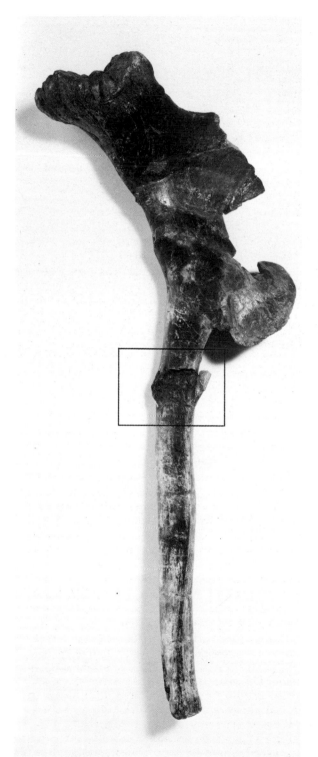

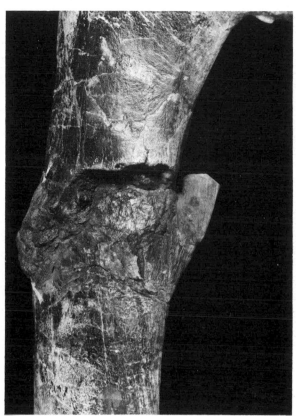

Left. A hip-bone (ischium) of an *Iguanodon*, broken during life and healed. Length 98 centimetres.
Above. An enlargement of the damaged area.

selves, within a species) and the marks of disease. The manner of their death can itself provide useful information.

As for the world in which they lived, a whole panorama can be built up from our knowledge of the other animals and plants with which they shared that world, of the sediments in which they were all buried and of other geological phenomena. A competent geologist can study those sediments and tell whether they were laid down in a hot or a cold climate, in wet or dry conditions, and whether or not there was much difference between the seasons of the year. An expert zoologist can obtain information on these subjects from the animals, a botanist from the plants. The more the items of information from various sources reinforce one another, the more can they be relied on.

9 · Principles of classification

Nobody knows how many animal species are living today, but it has been estimated (very roughly) that more than a million have been described and there are probably many times that number still awaiting description. Fossil species – nearly all of them unknown, of course – must number countless millions; even if we consider only the reptiles, the very small proportion that we actually know of, those alone must certainly run into several thousands. And dinosaurs must run into hundreds.

There are various practical reasons why all these species – like soldiers in an army, books in a library or stamps in a stamp collection – need to be listed or catalogued. True, they could be catalogued very simply in the alphabetical order of their names, or in numerical order according to the dates on which those names were first proposed; but such lists – while useful for certain purposes – would tell us nothing about the species themselves or their relationships to other species. Because these matters are extremely important (zoological studies are more often concerned with whole groups of species than with single isolated forms) we find it much more useful to classify our species according to their characters. The system employed is much the same as that used in a library, where books are classified and stored according to their subject. All the history books, for example, might be in one particular room; all the books on Greek history, Roman history, European history, English history, American history and so on would be kept in separate stacks within that room, and each shelf within each stack would be reserved for books on a particular period. Thus, if we wished to see all the literature on England in the sixteenth century, we should know exactly where to find it. There are, however, various differing ways of arranging the books in a library, not just one 'correct' way; which arrangement we choose is a matter of convenience and personal preference. And, however we do it, problems are bound to arise from time to time; some books could be placed equally appropriately on either of two shelves, maybe more than two, or they could even be housed in different rooms.

Likewise there are innumerable different ways in which animal species could be classified on shared characters; all classifications are *subjective*. The most useful way, however, is to classify the species according to their evolutionary relationships, on the objective phylogeny or 'family tree' on which all species can be placed. Indeed, all zoologists are agreed that the classification employed should be entirely consistent with the pattern of branching of that evolutionary tree, actually indicating the pattern of branching *as far as is practical and convenient*. But even with this strict limitation there are still many different formal classifications which, with varying degrees of success, can be used to represent such a tree (or part of it). No particular classification is 'correct' or 'incorrect', unless it violates all accepted views on the shape of the tree; most of the tree is entirely unknown, of course, but even if we knew it perfectly we should still be faced with the problem of taking a three-dimensional tree, branching irregularly, and representing it by a formal *hierarchical* classification on the two-dimensional pages of a book. (A hierarchical classification is one in which the objects concerned – in this case species – are arranged into graded categories of increasing size and importance, resembling the organization of soldiers into sections, platoons, companies, battalions, regiments, brigades, divisions and so on.) There are as many different ways of dividing up such an evolutionary tree into formal categories, each with its own advantages and disadvantages, as there are of sawing up a real tree into logs. And, even when we have decided which classification to use, we shall still find that many species – because of our imperfect knowledge of them – will fit equally well into any of two or more equivalent categories.

Incidentally, a formal classification of a group of species not only expresses the evolutionary relationships of those species but also

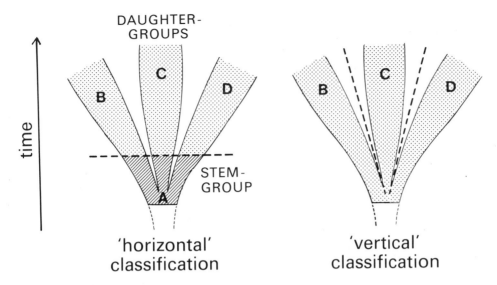

A simple diagram to illustrate the difference between 'horizontal' and 'vertical' classifications

helps us to *remember* that group (or any part of it in which we have a particular interest) and to make predictions about the species which it contains.

The fact that there are so many different ways of representing the evolutionary tree as a hierarchical classification has led to a great deal of controversy between systematists, often intense controversy, as to the best way of doing it. For example, where we have a new group breaking up into various daughter-groups (B, C, D) we may decide to designate a 'stem-group' (A) incorporating all the early forms (which are all quite closely related to each other, by a 'first-cousin' sort of relationship if not by direct ancestry); or, alternatively, we may try to do without a stem-group and assign all the early forms to the various daughter-groups. The former type of classification is referred to as 'horizontal', the latter as 'vertical', and systematists will never stop arguing as to their respective advantages and disadvantages. Alas, we cannot discuss this fascinating subject here because of limitations of space.

The different categories we use in our classification, the *taxa* (singular *taxon*), are themselves classified into grades. Obviously it would be cumbersome and impractical to have more than a few of these, and it has been generally agreed that there should be only four obligatory grades

between the *species* at the lower end of the scale and the *phylum*, one of the major divisions of the Animal Kingdom (like Molluscs, Arthropods and Chordates) at the upper. These obligatory grades, in order of increasing size, are *genus*, *family*, *order* and *class*. Thus the reptiles constitute a class Reptilia, within which there are sixteen orders; two of those, Saurischia and Ornithischia (collectively referred to as dinosaurs) each include several families, scores of genera and hundreds of species. It is often necessary, however, to insert additional grades between the obligatory grades, designating them by such names as subgenus, subfamily, superfamily, infraorder, superclass and so on. Terms such as 'tribe' may also be employed for this purpose.

The next larger grouping above the species is the genus; species are grouped into genera, but again the limits of the genus (especially in palaeontology) are a matter of opinion. When naming species we use the system of *binomial nomenclature* introduced by Linnaeus in 1753; the name must consist of two Latinized words, the first being the name of the genus to which the species is assigned (like *Diplodocus*) and the second being the particular name of the species itself (like *longus* or *carnegii*). Zoological nomenclature is no simple matter, being subject to an International Code of quasi-legal rules, complicated yet perfectly logical, and it is subject also to the jurisdiction of an International Commission of experts. Again, it is beyond the scope of this book to delve further into such a vast topic, interesting though it may be.

The classification of vertebrates – animals with backbones – was worked out originally on living forms; fossils were no more than an afterthought. (It must be remembered that this happened in the days when evolution was not even a respectable theory, let alone an accepted fact.) The same is true of other major animal groups. Indeed, it is very much easier to classify the animals of today if fossils are ignored; they were introduced only later into the classification and the problems that they have solved are outnumbered by the new ones that they have created.

Be that as it may, the vertebrates are divided into classes. The lower vertebrates, the fishes, are placed in classes of their own and do not concern us here. The higher vertebrates, comprising animals with four legs and with lungs for breathing air, are clearly divisible into four classes: Amphibians, Reptiles, Birds and Mammals. (Yes, it is true that birds and man have only two legs and snakes have none at all; but the birds have modified their front legs into wings, man uses his as arms, and the snakes – whose ancestors did possess four legs – have lost them altogether.) Each class has a whole set of characters by which it may be recognized. Thus a modern mammal, for example, does not lay eggs but brings forth its young alive, like miniature adults, to be fed by the mother on her milk and then looked after by one or both parents for some time longer. Mammals are 'warm-blooded' (i.e. the body temperature of more advanced mammals is always the same, about 37°C, no matter what the temperature may be outside) while reptiles are 'cold-blooded' (i.e., the temperature of the body goes up and down with the outside temperature). A mammal does not lose much heat to the surrounding air in cold weather because its body has a hairy covering (fur); a reptile, however, has no hair at all. The mammal heart has four compartments, the animal breathes by means of ribs and a muscular diaphragm, the brain is large, the lower jaw consists of only one bone on each side (the dentary), some of the other jaw bones have been incorporated into the sound-conducting mechanism of the middle ear, different parts of the mouth have different sorts of teeth, the teeth are replaced only once or not at all, there are ribs only in the front part of the body, the tail is usually very small and so on. In most of these features the mammal differs from nearly all reptiles.

We can therefore take any living four-legged backboned animal and tell very easily whether it is an amphibian, a reptile, a bird or a mammal. This happy situation has come about because the main branches of the evolutionary tree separated from each other long ago and are now quite distinct; each class represents all the twigs attached to one major branch of that tree. Indeed, there are very few living vertebrates which cause any problems at all. (One such problem animal is the duck-billed platypus which, although definitely a mammal – it suckles its young and has hair – does not produce its young alive but lays eggs like a reptile; to complicate matters further, it has a toothless bill like a bird's.)

Fossil vertebrates, however, are a very different matter. When they occur on the family tree near the point where one class branches off from another they are likely to show a mixture of modern class characters, or characters in a transitional condition. Thus, for example, we know that some 200 million years ago a certain line of reptiles (the 'mammal-like reptiles') evolved into mammals. We would not expect that the dozens of characters that differ in modern reptiles and mammals would all have changed from the reptile condition to the mammal condition at precisely the same time; rather should we expect them to have changed gradually, one by one over a long period, so that we should find fossil animals with a mixture of reptile and mammal characters. (In just the same way *Archaeopteryx*, to be discussed in Chapter 17, shows a mixture of reptile and bird characters.) This means that, if we also take fossil animals into consideration, the classes cannot be as distinct as they seem to be when we consider only the living forms. Even if we knew much more than we do know about the past history of life on earth, even if we knew all the details of the evolutionary tree, it would still be difficult to decide where each major branch ought to begin, and, therefore, to which class some of the earlier members ought to belong. Indeed, the fact that we do *not* know very much sometimes leaves us with gaps in the fossil record and makes it easier to choose a position for the boundary between successive taxa – easier than it would be if the record were continuous throughout.

It is in the nature of vertebrate fossils that they are frequently rather rare, so that in many cases we have only a single specimen, and very often the one or the few specimens that we do have are incomplete – perhaps only one bone, itself incomplete, out of an entire skeleton. It is also in their nature, in most cases, to consist of bones and teeth and nothing else. Therefore, from the point of view of the palaeontologist, the best class characters are bony characters, from those parts of the skeleton which are most often preserved (such as the exceptionally hard jaws and teeth of mammals). It is also desirable that a class character should be an 'all or nothing' character, something which is either present or absent, and not a character like 'warm-bloodedness' which can occur in an in-between condition. Thus, when considering the forms intermediate between reptiles and mammals, most palaeontologists are agreed that they should be called reptiles if the lower jaw has more than one bone on each side and mammals if the lower jaw has only the dentary; this character fulfils all the requirements mentioned above.

The fact that the living members of each class possess a well-defined set of class characters has one unfortunate consequence. We tend to forget that, way back down the family tree, there is a 'blurring' of the classes. Thus, when we decide (quite arbitrarily) that a certain intermediate fossil should be classified as, say, a reptile, we tend to assume unthinkingly that, when alive, it possessed all the characters of a modern reptile; this includes even the 'soft' characters, of which we have no direct evidence. Such an assumption, however, is quite unjustified and must often be wrong. We should therefore beware of this illogical, unscientific approach to

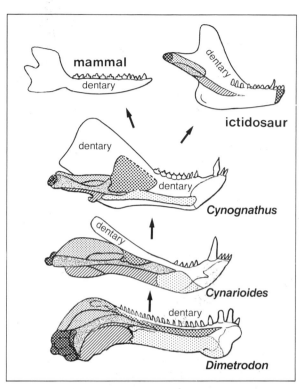

The inner sides of the lower jaws of a series of mammal-like reptiles (pelycosaur, gorgonopian, cynodont, ictidosaur); this shows the gradual increase in the size of the dentary at the expense of the other bones. The series ends with the lower jaw of a true mammal, consisting of dentary alone.

fossils, a good example of which is mentioned in Chapter 16.

Meanwhile in the next chapter (Chapter 10) we shall deal briefly with the general classification of the land vertebrates, in particular of the reptiles; we shall see how the dinosaurs fit into the reptile classification and how they themselves are classified. The classification used is fairly conventional, but it happens to be the one that we regard as the best at present available. Chapter 17, on the other hand, is partly concerned with a recent proposal that there should be major changes in the arrangement of vertebrates into classes, including a suggestion that the dinosaurs should be regarded, not as reptiles, but as a class of their own.

11 The ornithopod dinosaur *Lesothosaurus* (Early Jurassic, from southern Africa)

12 The carnosaur *Dilophosaurus* (Early Jurassic, from Arizona)

13 The parrot dinosaur *Psittacosaurus* (Early Cretaceous, from Mongolia)

14 The ornithopod dinosaur *Heterodontosaurus* (Early Jurassic, from southern Africa)

10 · Classification of dinosaurs

As noted above, we generally recognize four classes of tetrapods (four-limbed vertebrates): amphibians, reptiles, birds and mammals. The relationships between these classes are very simple; amphibians evolved from fishes and were ancestral to reptiles, which in turn gave rise to birds in one direction and to mammals in another. The reptiles therefore occupy a central position in the family tree and are of the greatest importance in any evolutionary study of vertebrate history.

Plate 15 is a very simple 'family tree' of the tetrapod classes and of the bony fishes from which they evolved, showing their inter-relationships. In order to make those relation-ships a little more explicit the 'fleshy-finned fishes' (Sarcopterygii), the amphibians and the reptiles have each been divided into three major components.

It was also mentioned in the previous chapter that, while the boundaries between the various classes are extremely clear when only their living members are considered, the classes nevertheless tend to grade into each other through fossil forms of intermediate nature.

Thus, for example, the distinction between modern fishes and modern amphibians is based upon – among other things – the amphibians' possession of limbs (with four or five toes). The same is true of the distinction between the ancient rhipidistian fishes and the primitive amphibians which evolved from them, where, because of lack of 'soft parts', this character is of even greater importance. But one isolated skull roof is known, intermediate in its pro-portions between fish and amphibian, which cannot be classified as either because we do not know whether the animal concerned was equip-ped with fins or limbs.

The distinction between amphibians and rep-tiles depends upon their method of reproduc-tion, presumed to have been the same in the fossil members of those classes as in the cor-responding modern representatives. Am-phibians generally lay their eggs ('spawn') in water; the eggs hatch into aquatic gill-breathing larvae ('tadpoles') and the larvae eventually metamorphose into terrestrial, mainly lung-breathing adults. Reptiles, by con-trast – except when viviparous – lay shelled

The skull roofs of:
(a) *Eusthenopteron*, a rhipidistian fish.
(b) *Elpistostege*, a little-known form seemingly intermediate in its proportions between A and C.
(c) *Ichthyostega*, a very early labyrinthodont amphibian. Corresponding bones are shaded alike.

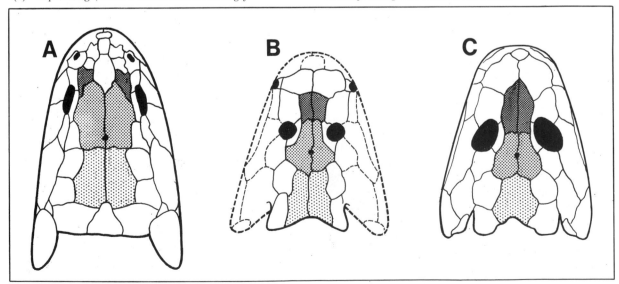

Tadpole of Common Frog (*Rana temporaria*)

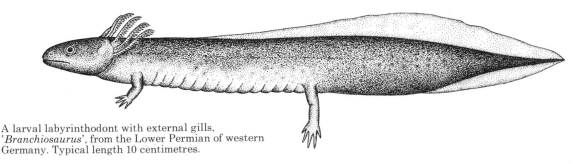

A larval labyrinthodont with external gills,
'*Branchiosaurus*', from the Lower Permian of western
Germany. Typical length 10 centimetres.

eggs which need air and must therefore be laid on land; the young that emerge from them are essentially miniature replicas of their parents. But, when considering the advanced amphibians and their early reptilian descendants, we have in most cases no direct information as to how they reproduced. In a few instances the gill-bearing larvae have actually been preserved as fossils, in others the form of the pelvis may give some indication as to the size of the egg laid. Less direct evidence, however, is afforded by the presence of grooves on the juvenile skull (suggesting that the animal possessed a so-called lateral-line system, used for sensing changes of pressure in the water), and we are generally forced to rely on other features of the skeleton that are supposed to be characteristic of either amphibians or reptiles.

When we come to the reptile-bird transition we regard the presence of feathers as the one really diagnostic feature of the birds – 'our feathered friends'. Fortunately for the systematist the one intermediate, the classic *Archaeopteryx* (discussed in detail in Chapter 17) is surrounded by the impressions of unmistakable feathers and is therefore classified quite positively as a bird. As for the transition from reptile to mammal, this has been considered earlier in Chapter 9 (pp.78 and 79).

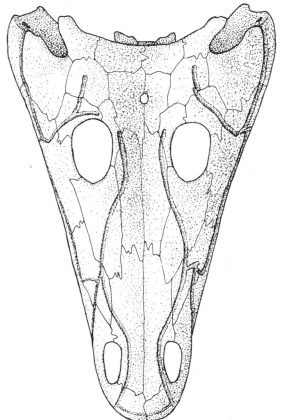

The skull of a labyrinthodont (*Benthosuchus*) from the lowest Triassic of Russia, showing the grooves for the lateral-line system. Length of skull 17 centimetres.

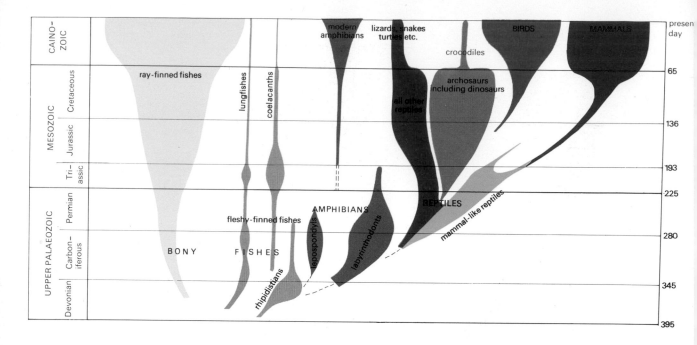

Top chart labels:

CAINOZOIC | Cretaceous | Jurassic | Tri-assic | Permian | Carbon-iferous | Devonian

MESOZOIC | UPPER PALAEOZOIC

ray-finned fishes
modern amphibians
lizards, snakes turtles etc.
BIRDS
MAMMALS
crocodiles
archosaurs including dinosaurs
lungfishes
coelacanths
all other reptiles
fleshy-finned fishes
AMPHIBIANS
REPTILES
mammal-like reptiles
lepospondyls
labyrinthodonts
BONY   FISHES
rhipidistians

present day | 65 | 136 | 193 | 225 | 280 | 345 | 395

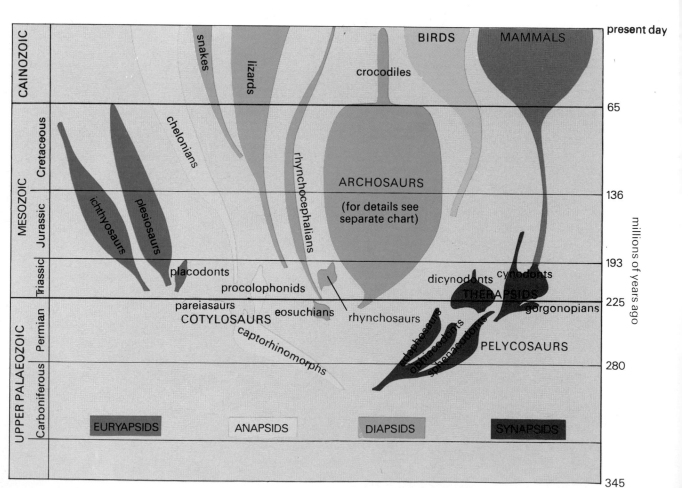

Bottom chart labels:

CAINOZOIC | MESOZOIC | UPPER PALAEOZOIC

Cretaceous | Jurassic | Triassic | Permian | Carboniferous

snakes
lizards
BIRDS
MAMMALS
crocodiles
chelonians
rhynchocephalians
ARCHOSAURS
(for details see separate chart)
ichthyosaurs
plesiosaurs
placodonts
procolophonids
dicynodonts
cynodonts
pareiasaurs
eosuchians
THERAPSIDS
COTYLOSAURS
rhynchosaurs
gorgonopians
captorhinomorphs
araeoscelids
ophiacodonts
sphenacodonts
PELYCOSAURS

EURYAPSIDS | ANAPSIDS | DIAPSIDS | SYNAPSIDS

present day | 65 | 136 | 193 | 225 | 280 | 345

millions of years ago

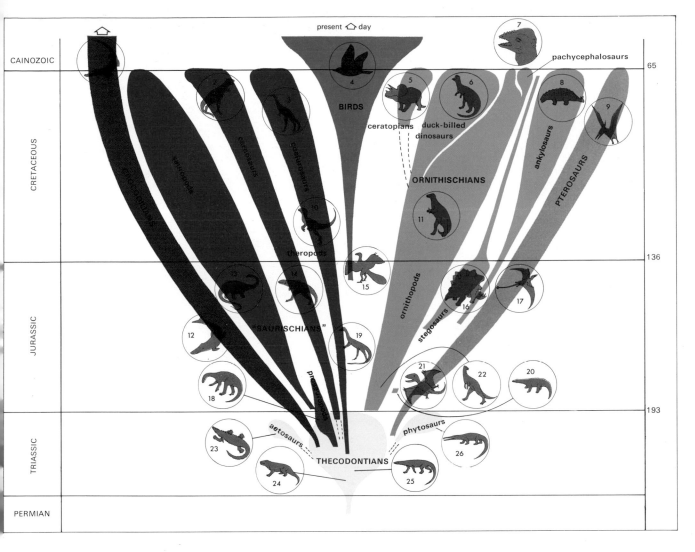

CAINOZOIC

present ⌂ day

pachycephalosaurs

BIRDS

ceratopians

duck-billed
dinosaurs

ORNITHISCHIANS

ankylosaurs

PTEROSAURS

crocodilians

sauropods

coelurosaurs

theropods

ornithopods

stegosaurs

"SAURISCHIANS"

prosauropods

aetosaurs

phytosaurs

THECODONTIANS

CRETACEOUS

JURASSIC

TRIASSIC

PERMIAN

65

136

193

17 *Above*. The family tree of the archosaurs

This diagram is rather more conservative than the
text, in that the dromaeosaurids (such as *Deinonychus*) are included within the coelurosaurs instead of being regarded as part of a separate grouping, the deinonychosaurs.

1 Modern crocodile
2 *Tyrannosaurus*
3 *Ornithomimus*
4 Modern bird
5 *Triceratops*
6 *Corythosaurus*
7 *Pachycephalosaurus*
8 *Euoplocephalus*
9 *Pteranodon*
10 *Deinonychus*
11 *Iguanodon*
12 *Metriorhynchus*
13 *Diplodocus*

14 *Megalosaurus*
15 *Archaeopteryx*
16 *Stegosaurus*
17 *Rhamphorhynchus*
18 *Plateosaurus*
19 *Coelophysis*
20 *Scelidosaurus*
21 *Dimorphodon*
22 *Lesothosaurus*
23 *Desmatosuchus*
24 *Erythrosuchus*
25 *Mandasuchus*
26 *Rutiodon*

15 *Above left*. A greatly simplified 'family tree' of the land
vertebrates (tetrapods) and of the bony fishes from which
they evolved. The amphibians and the fleshy-finned fishes
are shown in a little more detail.

16 *Below left*. The family tree of the reptiles

So much for the tetrapod classes. Within the class Reptilia there are a number of orders (somewhat variable, depending on which particular authority is followed, but generally about sixteen) and these are grouped into four *subclasses* according to the arrangement of the temporal openings in the side of the skull behind the eye. As mentioned in Chapter 1, those openings lighten the skull without weakening it and, in addition, allow room for the bulging of the jaw muscles. The *anapsids* possess no openings at all; the *diapsids* possess two, an upper and a lower, separated by a bar which is formed from a backward projection of the postorbital bone and a forward projection of the squamosal. The *synapsids* (all extinct) had only one opening, which must have been the lower of the two because the two bones mentioned met above it; the *euryapsids* also possessed only one, but that had to be the upper because the same two bones met *below* it. (The basic pattern characteristic of each subclass was often modified to some extent in its later, more advanced members.) The family tree of the various reptile groups and of the birds and mammals descended from them is better shown graphically (Plate 16) than described in words; this tree indicates the interrelationships, as far as we know them, and the colour-coding shows to which of the four subclasses the various groups belong.

In one respect, however, this family tree of the reptiles is not detailed enough for our purpose. It shows one great division of the diapsids as the *archosaurs* ('ruling reptiles') which in fact constitute a superorder embracing five separate orders and including all the dinosaurs. We therefore give a separate family tree of the archosaurs alone in much greater detail (Plate 17). This shows very clearly how the most primitive archosaurs are regarded as a 'stem-order', the Thecodontia, from which evolved four 'daughter-orders': the Crocodilia (including the modern crocodiles), the Pterosauria (or winged reptiles, including the pterodactyls), the Saurischia and the Ornithischia. At this point we must recall our definition of a dinosaur from Chapter 1 and that, although we do tend to think of the Saurischia and Ornithischia together as constituting a single group of animals, they are usually regarded by palaeontologists

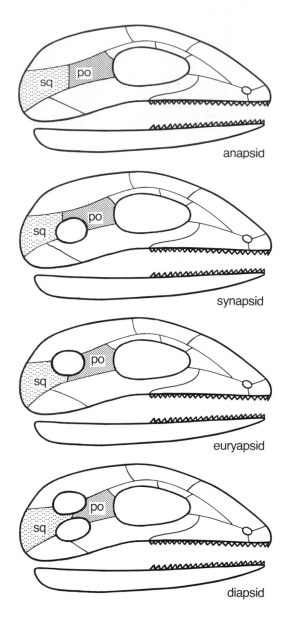

The four basic types of reptile skull pattern.
po postorbital; sq squamosal.

as two separate orders which differ from each other in several ways; all known dinosaurs fall very definitely into one order or the other. (In apparent contradiction to this, it has been claimed as recently as 1974 that the Saurischia and the Ornithischia *did* share a common ancestor which was not ancestral to anything else and that those two separate orders should therefore be reunited as the Dinosauria. This could indeed be true, but – we repeat – no palaeontologist has yet produced any convincing evidence suggesting that the Saurischia and the Ornithischia were more closely related to each other than is either to any of the other archosaur daughter-groups such as the Crocodilia or the Pterosauria. In fact, it is even possible that the Saurischia themselves originated from the Thecodontia as two or more separate groups.) This brief explanation, in conjunction with the two family trees, should show with sufficient clarity how the dinosaurs are fitted into the general framework of reptilian classification.

What is the basic difference between the two dinosaurian orders? In the Saurischia, the 'lizard-hipped' dinosaurs, the bones of the hip region are not very different from those of many other reptiles: one of the bones beneath the hip-socket, the pubis, points downwards and forwards, while the other, the ischium, points downwards and backwards. In the Ornithischia, however, the 'bird-hipped' dinosaurs, the bones of the hip region are very different from those of all other reptiles and, at first sight, are more like those of birds. The pubis no longer points downwards and forwards but has swung back to a position beneath the ischium; just like the ischium, it now points downwards and *backwards*. (In most ornithischians the pubis has also developed a new branch pointing forwards.) Anyone visiting the Dinosaur Gallery in a large museum should have no difficulty in deciding which of the dinosaurs belongs to the Saurischia and which to the Ornithischia; all that is needed is one glance at their hip-bones (*see* p.90).

As for the many other differences between the two orders, in nearly every case it is the ornithischian which has developed some special characters; it is the saurischian which remains more 'ordinary' like other reptiles. For example, in all backboned animals except ornithischians the main bone of the lower jaw on each side, the dentary, is joined in the mid-line to the other dentary to form the end of the chin. Saurischians too are like this. In ornithischians, however, there is a single middle bone called the predentary capping the two dentaries; it is the predentary which forms the point

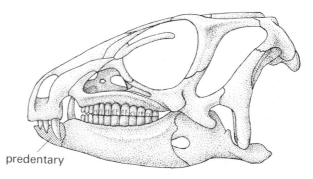

predentary

The skull of *Heterodontosaurus*, an ornithopod from the Upper Trias of southern Africa, to show the characteristic predentary bone. Length of skull 9 centimetres.

of the chin. *All* ornithischians have a predentary, but no other reptile has one. Again, in ornithischians the neural spines of the vertebrae (which in human beings form the row of knobs on the backbone, down the middle of the back) are connected to each other by a bony lattice-work. This too is not found in saurischians. A final point, already mentioned, is that the ornithischians were all plant-eaters, whereas many of the saurischians still ate meat.

The classification of dinosaurs extends far beyond a simple division into saurischians and ornithischians (*see* Plate 17). The saurischians are themselves divided into theropods and sauropodomorphs. The theropods, very distinctive dinosaurs, walked only on their back legs, and almost all were flesh-eaters. (Nearly all other dinosaurs, by contrast, ate nothing but plants.) The sauropodomorphs include the familiar *Brontosaurus* and *Diplodocus* and all their relatives.

18 *Overleaf.* Western North America during the Late Cretaceous. (It is not certain that all dinosaurs shown here lived in exactly the same place at exactly the same time.) In the foreground an ostrich dinosaur (*Ornithomimus*) runs towards the left, while the armoured *Euoplocephalus* moves in the opposite direction. Farther back the great carnosaur *Tyrannosaurus* adopts a threatening posture and is clearly intending to attack one of the two large herbivores in the middle distance, either the flat-headed duckbill (*Anatosaurus*) in front or the domehead (*Pachycephalosaurus*) behind. In the background the horned *Triceratops* trots unconcernedly across the landscape.

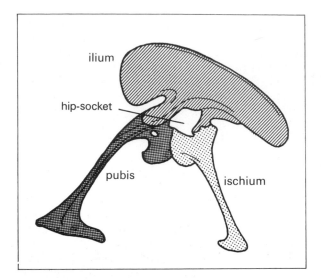

The hip-bones of the saurischian dinosaur *Ceratosaurus*. In this diagram, as in the other two, the bones are viewed from the outer side.

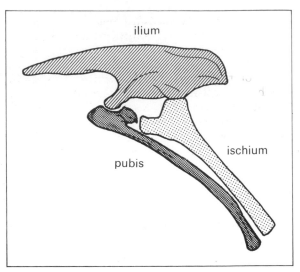

The hip-bones of the early ornithischian *Scelidosaurus*

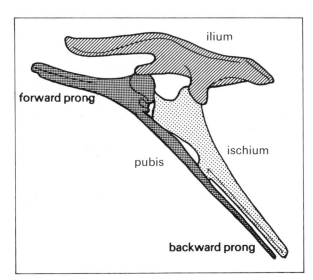

The hip-bones of the later, 'typical' ornithischian *Thescelosaurus*.

Part of the backbone of an *Iguanodon*, showing the bony lattice-work (ossified tendons) connecting the neural spines of the vertebrae

Even the theropods can be divided further. The coelurosaurs were lightly built animals with small heads, long necks and fairly well developed fore-limbs; they were generally small, but some attained quite impressive dimensions in Cretaceous times. The carnosaurs, by contrast, were much larger and more heavily built, with relatively large heads, short necks, and front legs much reduced. Not everyone is convinced, however, that we are correct in making this simple division, for some of the medium-sized theropods seem to show a mixture of characters intermediate between those of coelurosaurs and carnosaurs with others quite distinct from either; in fact, a new school of thought favours the recognition of a third group of theropods, the deinonychosaurs, in which the skull and limbs are highly specialized for fast movement and savage attack.

The sauropodomorphs can likewise be divided into two. The more important subdivision is the sauropods, which are the gigantic plant-eating quadrupeds such as *Diplodocus*; they had small heads, long necks, very long tails and elephantine legs, and they include the largest animals that ever lived on land. Less important are the prosauropods, earlier in time than the sauropods and once thought to be their ancestors but now regarded as a parallel, shorter-lived offshoot from a common stock. They were smaller than the sauropods, somewhat similar in general form but not so extreme; some of them could probably get up on their back legs when the fancy took them, and some of the earlier ones may still have preferred a diet of meat to eating plants.

The second order of dinosaurs consists of the ornithischians or 'bird-hipped' forms. Despite their name and the shape of their hip-bones, these dinosaurs are not especially close relatives of the birds; indeed, as we shall see later (Chapter 17), most people now believe that the birds evolved from the *saurischian* dinosaurs.

Whereas the primary subdivision of the saurischians is into only two, the ornithischians are usually divided into four. The most abundant group was the Ornithopoda, all of which showed a tendency towards bipedality. But these ornithopods, although obviously capable of walking on their back legs alone, were probably quadrupedal on occasions; some of them may have preferred to spend more time on only two legs, others may have preferred to use all four. In this they differed from the theropods mentioned above; the theropods *never* used their front legs for walking. The ornithopods also differed from the meat-eating theropods in that, like all other ornithischians, they ate only plants; the only known exception to that rule is *Troodon* (*see* p.17).

One very important and specialized branch of the ornithopods, important because of their great abundance, was the hadrosaurs or duck-billed dinosaurs. Much rarer and therefore much less important were the pachycephalosaurs or dome-headed dinosaurs.

The other three groups of ornithischian dinosaurs – the horned, the plated, and the armoured dinosaurs – were all completely quadrupedal; unlike the ornithopods they could not stand or walk on their back legs alone. They were nevertheless quite unrelated to each other, except, of course, in so far as they were all 'bird-hipped' dinosaurs (and therefore plant-eaters). In fact, the horned dinosaurs – ceratopians, often wrongly called ceratopsians – were almost certainly more closely related to the partly bipedal ornithopods than they were to the plated dinosaurs (stegosaurs) or armoured dinosaurs (ankylosaurs). They may even have descended from the ornithopods via something like the parrot dinosaurs (*see* Chapter 14), losing their generally two-legged posture and returning completely to all fours.

We have now set the scene with our outline classification of the dinosaurs and can soon get down to describing a representative selection of these remarkable creatures.

19 The deinonychosaur *Deinonychus* (Early Cretaceous,
from Montana)

11 · Origin of dinosaurs

We have already established in Chapter 4 that the dinosaurs lived in Late Triassic, Jurassic and Cretaceous times and that the mammal-like reptiles preceded them as the dominant vertebrates on land. Chapter 10 explained the general scheme of reptilian classification, how the archosaurs fit into it, how the archosaurs themselves are classified into orders and how the two dinosaur orders are split up into smaller groups. But what has not yet been made clear is why the dinosaurs and other higher archosaurs arose

when they did and how they managed to replace the mammal-like reptile and mammal line as the most important and successful group of large land-dwelling vertebrates. After all, the archosaurs were mere reptiles and should therefore have been greatly inferior to the contemporary mammals!

The figure below shows how the comparative fortunes of the two great groups under discussion have waxed and waned from Carboniferous times to the present day. The diagram, of

A rough guide to the relative fortunes since the Carboniferous of the mammal-like reptiles and their descendants on the one hand, and of the archosaurs and their descendants on the other

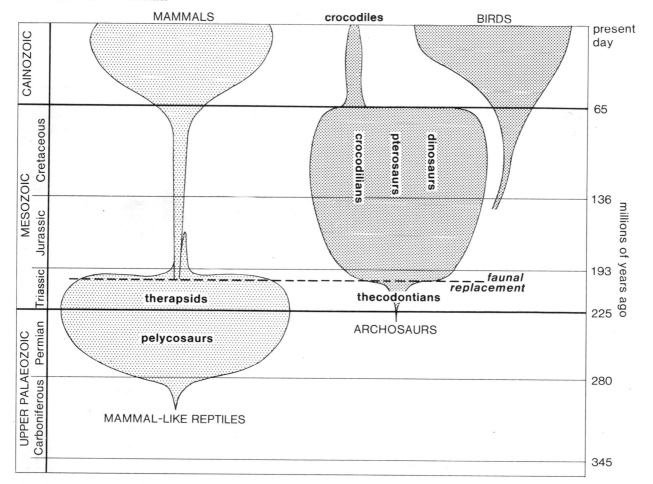

Paracyclotosaurus, one of the last of the labyrinthodonts, from the Upper Trias of New South Wales. Length about 2.25 metres.

course, is very much simplified; none of the other major groups, such as amphibians or lizards, is represented at all, but they are relatively unimportant in this connection. It does show, however, that the archosaurs took over from the mammal-like reptiles about two-thirds of the way through Triassic time, that the early mammals remained small and unimportant throughout the whole of the Mesozoic, and that the mammals were eventually able to stage a come-back but only *after* the dinosaur extinction at the end of the Cretaceous. Let us now attempt to trace the broad outlines of the history of the tetrapods (i.e., the four-limbed vertebrates – amphibians, reptiles, birds and mammals), focussing our attention almost exclusively upon the Triassic period; such a history should help us to understand the evolution of the various major groups during this important segment of geological time and also to understand their effects upon each other.

We shall begin by looking at the tetrapods' family tree. To be more precise, we must look at *three* evolutionary trees, Plates 15–17; Plate 15 is a very simple family tree of *all* the tetrapods, Plate 16 gives the reptiles in greater detail but still shows the Archosauria collectively as a single undivided mass, and Plate 17 is therefore necessary if we wish to see how the stem archosaurs evolved into smaller subordinate units. Of particular interest to us is the fact that this last tree shows us the origin of the dinosaurs; it indicates that the basal order ('stem-

order') of the archosaurs was the Thecodontia, and that the dinosaurs, as we have defined them in this book, appear to have arisen from the Thecodontia in Triassic times as two distinct daughter-orders – the Saurischia and the Ornithischia.

While studying this composite family tree, however, we notice something else even more interesting – something really quite remarkable. For it is abundantly clear that all the major tetrapod groups which lived in the Palaeozoic – in the Late Carboniferous and the Permian – virtually died out during the Triassic; they comprise the various sorts of ancient amphibians (including the big labyrinthodonts that lived in the coal forests of the Carboniferous period), a number of large and important groups of the most primitive reptiles of all (collectively called the cotylosaurs) and, last but by no means least, many different groups of mammal-like reptiles or synapsids. A couple of groups did linger on into the Jurassic, but only in insignificant numbers.

It is equally clear that all the tetrapod groups which dominated the continents during the Mesozoic, all those that returned to the Mesozoic seas, and, in addition, all those that have survived to the present day, made their first effective appearance in Triassic or earliest Jurassic times. The exclusively Mesozoic land reptiles were the saurischian dinosaurs, the ornithischian dinosaurs and the pterosaurs, all of which first enter the fossil record at the times just mentioned. The Mesozoic sea reptiles comprise the plesiosaurs and the ichthyosaurs, together with a couple of lesser-known and shorter-lived groups. The groups which, after their Early Mesozoic début, have survived up to the present are the frogs, testudinates (turtles and tortoises), lizards, crocodiles and of course the mammals. It must be admitted that the lizards might have appeared a little earlier than the others – in the Late Permian – but they are found there only in small numbers and in an only partly evolved condition; indeed, whether or not those Late Permian forms should be called lizards in the strict sense is a matter of opinion. More important, it is also true that one or two modern groups did not originate until rather later – the birds not until later in the Jurassic, the snakes not until

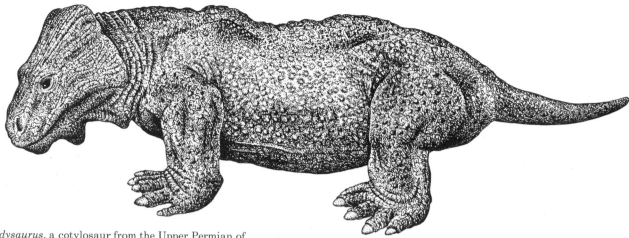

Bradysaurus, a cotylosaur from the Upper Permian of
South Africa. Typical length 2.2 metres.

the Early Cretaceous; but, with the possible
exception of the former and the certain exception of the latter (and, after all, snakes are
really nothing more than highly specialized
lizards) no entirely new groups of land vertebrates have originated since the earliest Jurassic, nearly 200 million years ago.

Thus it would seem that the land vertebrates
of the Palaeozoic (which we may for convenience call palaeotetrapods) were almost
completely replaced during the Triassic period
by entirely new groups (which we shall collectively refer to as neotetrapods). This replacement, which was most apparent among the
larger animals, happened gradually but with
ever-increasing tempo, culminating in a final
phase of very rapid change at the end of Middle
Triassic and the beginning of Late Triassic
times. The most conspicuous of the palaeotetrapods were the mammal-like reptiles; the dominant neotetrapods for the rest of the Mesozoic era were, as their name implies, the
archosaurs or 'ruling reptiles', especially the
dinosaurs, and after the end of the Mesozoic the
most important land vertebrates were the mammals and the birds.

We should naturally expect the neotetrapods
to have progressed farther along the evolutionary road than had the palaeotetrapods, to
be superior to them in their anatomy and
physiology. This expectation is not only realized but greatly exceeded. For the neotetrapods
were not merely more advanced than the

palaeotetrapods; they were altogether – to use a
footballing analogy – in a higher division of the
league. The palaeotetrapods, even though they
had dominated the land unchallenged for some
120 million years and lived in competition with
the neotetrapods for another 30 million, even
though they comprised an enormous number of
very different species, were essentially ultra-
conservative in their structure and habits. They
were nearly all land-dwelling quadrupedal
'sprawlers'; indeed, the only really significant
modifications evolved by any reptiles in all that
time were those connected with herbivory,
those modifications of the jaws and teeth (and
presumably also of the digestive system) which
would enable them to make use of the vast
quantities of vegetation that must have been
available during the Late Palaeozoic. Thus,

Temnodontosaurus, an ichthyosaur from the Lower
Jurassic of England. Length up to 9 metres or even more.

Kuehneosaurus, a gliding
lizard from the Upper Trias
of Somerset. Typical length
75 centimetres.

while it is true that some of the later, more advanced mammal-like reptiles had begun to improve their limb posture, it would seem that none of the palaeotetrapods was a particularly good runner, and it is certain that none developed bipedality; they showed no adaptations for climbing nor did the early reptiles lose their limbs to become burrowers. The palaeotetrapods were never very large – not much bigger than a cow. None (as far as we know) was warm-blooded, and only the fin-backs like *Dimetrodon* appear to have been equipped with any sort of device for maintaining the body at a temperature different from that of the surrounding air. None possessed any offensive or defensive weapons other than teeth; none had a protective shell or a complete covering of armour plates, although a few palaeotetrapods did develop a certain amount of bony plating in the skin. No palaeotetrapod above the amphibian grade ever returned to a wholly aquatic life in fresh water (one or two were semi-aquatic) and, except for one family of Early Triassic amphibians, no palaeotetrapod of any sort ever took to life in the sea. Finally, none took to the air, except perhaps for some small Permian forms with gliding membranes borne on extended ribs.

By contrast, all the various progressive trends in evolution which the palaeotetrapods had failed to initiate were made by some or other of the newly evolved neotetrapods, in every case during Triassic time. The neotetrapods improved their stance and gait, pulling their limbs into a more upright position beneath the body to become at first 'semi-erect' (e.g. thecodontians, crocodiles, primitive mammals) and then 'fully erect' (e.g. dinosaurs; birds and more advanced mammals later); the 'fully erect' forms were almost invariably digitigrade, walking always on their toes. Such animals were able to run well and often evolved further to become true bipeds (e.g. many dinosaurs, birds). The improved limb posture also enabled the animals (e.g. some dinosaurs) to grow to gigantic dimensions which, mechanically and dynamically, would have been impossible for terrestrial 'sprawlers'. Some neotetrapods became jumpers (the thecodontian *Scleromochlus*), gliders (some lizards, pterosaurs) and active fliers (birds; later bats; perhaps also pterosaurs). The more active lives which these creatures led must also have required a more advanced physiology, a system capable of producing more energy more rapidly; and, although we cannot know such things for certain, we can guess that some sort of control over body temperature developed in some neotetrapods fairly early in their history. (This could have been facilitated by insulation of the body – feathers, fur, or fat under the skin – and also by very large size.) Improvements in teeth and jaws, especially in ornithischian dinosaurs, sometimes paralleled or even exceeded those found in mammal-like reptiles.

Many neotetrapods were equipped with offensive weapons and protective devices, such as horns, whip-lash tail, or a tail with spikes or a club at the end (as in various dinosaurs). Some of them evolved complete armour-plating or 'shells' for protection (turtles, placodonts, aëtosaurs, ankylosaurian dinosaurs). Others returned to the waters from which their amphibian ancestors had originally emerged; they became semi-aquatic in fresh water (crocodiles, phytosaurs), frequented sea-shores and coastal shallows (nothosaurs, placodonts) or lived in the open oceans (plesiosaurs and ichthyosaurs). The ichthyosaurs, indeed, were so completely adapted to a fully marine existence that they were quite unable to come back on shore; their limbs, more like fins than legs, could hardly have supported them on land.

At this point we shall find it instructive to take a closer look at the stages in which the faunal replacement occurred. In the Early Triassic the large animals of the land were still – as in the preceding Late Permian – almost exclusively mammal-like reptiles; by far the most

Henodus, a placodont from the Upper Trias of Germany. Typical length just over 1 metre.

A more detailed chart of the major groups of land reptiles just before, during, and just after the Triassic; these include not only the therapsids (advanced mammal-like reptiles) and the archosaurs but also the rhynchosaurs

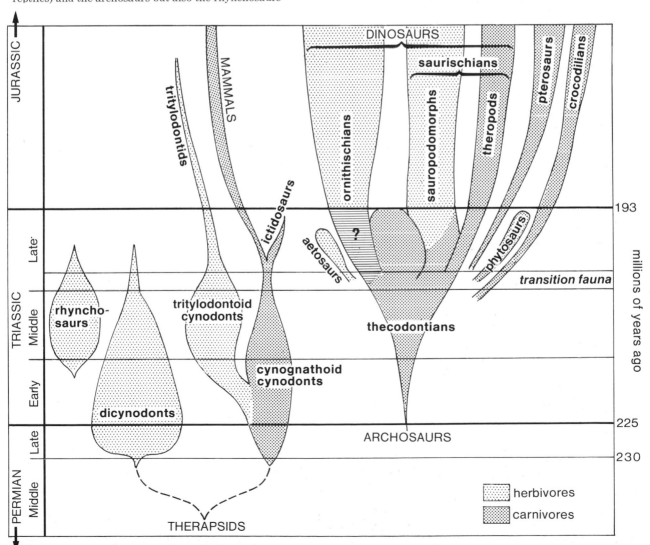

Nothosaurus, a nothosaur from the Middle and Upper Trias of Europe, Israel and elsewhere. Length up to 3 metres.

numerous of these were the many different dicynodonts, up to the size of a rhinoceros, some of which had only a pair of tusk-like upper canine teeth while others had no teeth at all. This lack of teeth suggests that the dicynodonts sliced up plants with the horny bill that doubtless covered their jaws in life; their great abundance too might be construed as evidence of herbivorous habits, for herbivores normally constitute the greater part of any balanced population. They were, indeed, the first group in vertebrate history to make effective use of all the plant food growing on the land and to become spectacularly successful as vegetarians. The main carnivorous element in the mammal-like reptile population, the cynognathoid cynodonts, have already been encountered elsewhere in this book (p.37); just like modern mammals, they had teeth which were already differentiated into incisors, canines and cheek teeth, and they must have fed very largely upon their dicynodont cousins. Although not nearly as numerous as the latter, the cynodonts were just as varied; the largest species known must have been nearly 2 metres in length. In the

Lystrosaurus, a dicynodont from the Lower Trias of South Africa. Typical length 1 metre.

later part of the Early Triassic a new type of cynodont appeared, the tritylodontoids, in which the teeth were rather different and obviously more suitable for cutting up plant material than for killing and eating other animals. The only other large creatures in the Early Triassic faunas – the only ones which were *not* mammal-like reptiles – were the earliest archosaurs, primitive thecodontians which were still clumsy 'sprawlers' but which were entirely carnivorous; their teeth, however, were entirely different from the mammal-like teeth of the cynodonts, for they were all (except in size) more or less the same: set in sockets, sharply pointed, curved slightly backwards, and frequently a little flattened so that a ridge separated the surface on the lip side from the surface on the mouth side. The ridge itself was often serrated like a steak-knife. Some of these thecodontians grew quite large; one of them, *Erythrosuchus* from South Africa, had a skull nearly a metre long and is the largest animal known to have existed on land before Late Triassic times. These earliest archosaurs were still exceedingly rare.

Skull of the cynodont *Cynognathus crateronotus*, from the Lower Trias of South Africa; 40 centimetres long, it is the largest cynodont skull known

Chasmatosaurus, a very primitive thecodontian from the Lower Trias of South Africa and elsewhere. Typical length 1.5 metres.

Erythrosuchus, a primitive thecodontian from the Lower Trias of South Africa. Typical length 4.5 metres.

In essence, then, a typical Early Triassic fauna consisted of dicynodonts and tritylodontoid cynodonts eating plants – probably different sorts of plants – and, in turn, being eaten by cynognathoid cynodonts and a very few primitive thecodontians.

A typical Middle Triassic fauna was characterized by a new group of large herbivorous reptiles, the rhynchosaurs, which were neither mammal-like reptiles nor archosaurs but were distant relatives of the lizards. It also included, however, the same four groups listed above for the Early Triassic, albeit with certain changes. Among the herbivores, the tritylodontoid cynodonts were much more numerous than in Early Triassic times (their teeth having become more specialized towards a vegetarian diet) and the

Stenaulorhynchus, a rhynchosaur from the Middle Trias of Tanzania

dicynodonts were correspondingly fewer. The carnivorous cynodonts (cynognathoids) were also less abundant and seemingly rather smaller. As for the thecodontians, their limb posture had by now attained the 'semi-improved' condition; and, although they were not yet numerous as individuals, they were already represented by many different species – in other words, they had diversified to a great extent. Nevertheless they were all still carnivorous, with the typical thecodontian teeth as described above. And some were very large, larger than any of the other elements in the faunal assemblage.

The differences which we have just noted, however, between the Early and Middle Triassic faunas are insignificant when compared with the dramatic differences between those of Middle and Late Triassic times. Of the five main groups in the Middle Triassic fauna, four had been greatly reduced by the Late Triassic: the dicynodonts had disappeared almost entirely (leaving but one surviving genus in western North America), both the carnivorous and the herbivorous cynodont stocks had become highly specialized and very rare, and even the rhynchosaurs were no longer so abundant. The carnivorous cynodonts, incidentally, also gave origin at the end of the Triassic to the first tiny mammals. But the sad decline of those four once great groups was in striking contrast to the rising fortunes of the archosaurs, which had suddenly evolved explosively and now constituted the greater part of the fauna. Some still possessed the 'semi-improved' limb posture and

should therefore still be classified as thecodontians; the majority, however, had become 'fully improved' and must therefore be regarded as dinosaurs, exclusively (or almost exclusively) saurischian dinosaurs. Some of them, even when they first appeared in the Late Triassic, were already habitual bipeds. The first saurischians known, in fact, were either small, lightly built bipedal carnivores (coelurosaurs) or larger, sometimes enormous prosauropods which often tended strongly towards herbivory and sometimes a little towards bipedality. Moreover, in addition to the 'typical' thecodontians and the various saurischians, four other new groups of archosaurs had become firmly established by Late Triassic times. Two of these, the phytosaurs and the aetosaurs, are considered to be specialized suborders of the order Thecodontia, dying out at the end of the Triassic; the other two, the crocodilians and the pterosaurs, are always regarded as fully independent orders of the Archosauria, persisting to the present day and to the end of the Mesozoic respectively. The phytosaurs (*see* figure above) were heavily armoured, rather crocodile-like in their appearance and also, most probably, in their habits, the aetosaurs (*see* figure adjacent) were similar, even more heavily armoured, but they were thorough-going land-dwellers and were either herbivorous (like the ornithischians and some prosauropods) or, at least, omnivorous in their diet.

Rutiodon, a phytosaur from the Upper Trias of North Carolina. Typical length 3.6 metres.

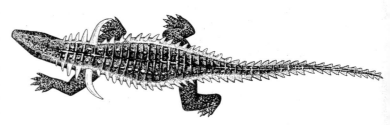

Desmatosuchus, an aetosaur from the Upper Trias of Texas. Typical length 3 metres.

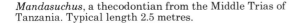

Mandasuchus, a thecodontian from the Middle Trias of Tanzania. Typical length 2.5 metres.

Thus, to sum up, the transition from Middle to Late Triassic times is marked by two concurrent and related phenomena. One is the sudden decline of the rhynchosaurs and of all the different groups of mammal-like reptiles; the other is the almost unbelievable increase and radiation of the archosaurs to fill every available niche, both for herbivores and for carnivores, in the new faunal assemblage. At the same time, as we have seen above, several other new groups of higher vertebrates made their first appearance, in the sea as well as on land and in the air – groups like the testudinates (turtles and tortoises), the plesiosaurs and – a little later – the mammals.

Only one fauna is known which actually shows the change-over taking place. In western Argentina the Ischigualasto Formation contains what looks like a Middle Triassic assemblage, with mammal-like reptiles still present in fair abundance; but it also includes two primitive aetosaurs, what may be an early crocodile, a few saurischian dinosaurs and (rather doubtfully) one ornithischian – the only Triassic ornithischian known, if it does indeed belong to that order.

This raises an interesting question: what about the ornithischians? The present chapter is entitled 'Origin of dinosaurs', but only saurischians have been mentioned up to now. Frankly, we do not know the answer. Apart from the one enigmatic fossil just referred to, the earliest ornithischians are in Lower Jurassic rocks. Some experts are of the opinion that they originated from thecodontians, independently of all other dinosaurs; a minority belief is that they evolved from the prosauropods, but as yet we have no proof either for or against what is, to my mind, a mere conjecture.

Up to now we have been dealing with facts, or at least with facts as revealed by the fossil record. It must be admitted that the record is very incomplete and often dated inaccurately; even so, no one could deny that four of the five reptile groups which are found so abundantly in Middle Triassic deposits are extremely rare or totally lacking in Upper Triassic beds. Likewise it cannot be denied that the fifth group, the archosaurs, are comparatively rare in the Middle Trias yet enormously abundant in the Upper. In summary, we cannot deny this drastic and fundamental change in the nature of the vertebrate land fauna, or that many new adaptations, many new life-styles appeared in the latter half of the Triassic period. But why did it happen at all, why did it produce such great diversity, and why was it (in a geological sense) so sudden and simultaneous?

At this point the facts will end and the speculation will begin. However, we hope that the explanation offered is an intelligent one; it is at least simple and logical, and it is difficult to think of another. Let us consider the Middle Triassic thecodontians – creatures with limb posture more highly improved than that of other contemporary reptiles, perhaps with physiology to match and presumably very active, wholly carnivorous, extremely varied and evolving rapidly; and, most important, some of them (the Prestosuchidae) were bigger than any other land animals of the time, probably thanks to the improved limb posture. And it was the descendants of this group that inherited the land after the change-over. Does it not seem very likely that they were the cause of the change?

The thecodontians, like all the competing reptile stocks, were constantly evolving improvements to their structure and physiology. It would seem that, by Middle Triassic times, some of them had reached a level of organization, a threshold – it might well have been attained by members of another group but it just so happened that certain thecodontians were the first to reach it – at which they were able to dominate the other groups to an extent that had never been known before. Other carnivores found themselves competing unsuccessfully with the great thecodontians for the diminishing supplies of meat, and herbivores were harried without respite; indeed, the great carnivorous thecodontians were such successful predators that they eventually brought about the decline and extinction of the animals on which they preyed and likewise of the other carnivores with which they were competing. Meanwhile their activities enhanced the effects of natural selection and increased the 'selection pressure' on all those other species, including many of their fellow thecodontians; it was a case of 'evolve or die'. 'Normal' individuals in each affected species had but greatly reduced chances of survival, whereas individuals possessing advantageous variations were more favourably placed. When those variations were heritable, i.e. when they could be passed on to the next generation, the proportion of individuals possessing them gradually increased. Other groups within the fauna, even other thecodontians, began to evolve more rapidly; this enabled them, for the first time, to overcome the enormous difficulties involved in the adoption of new habits and the colonization of new habitats. In those new habitats, empty of tetrapod life until then, they were able to evolve even more quickly and to fill all the available ecological niches – in other words, to undergo an almost 'explosive' radiation.

Most of the mammal-like reptiles died out; a few tiny ones found a new way of life, perhaps nocturnal or burrowing, and became the first mammals. Other groups, as we have seen, escaped the holocaust by taking to the waters or the air. And some of the thecodontians themselves (not necessarily the ones that were producing the selection pressure) evolved in various directions to fill the vacancies which the mammal-like reptiles and the other groups had left in the fauna of large terrestrial vertebrates. The keen competition for meat and the near-disappearance of the other plant-eaters (dicynodonts, tritylodontoid cynodonts, rhynchosaurs) led to the evolution of herbivorous archosaurs – an entirely new development. These herbivorous archosaurs were able to survive the onslaught of their predatory cousins because of their new adaptations: protective armour (aëtosaurs), fast bipedal running (ornithischian

dinosaurs) or large size (prosauropod dinosaurs). The carnivorous archosaurs were obliged to imitate them in evolving bipedal running (all theropod dinosaurs) and large size (carnosaurs); some of them, in addition, acquired exceptionally large heads with teeth to match and, if bipeds, powerful grasping hands. Thus there came into existence the first of the varied dinosaur faunas that were to rule the land for the rest of the Mesozoic era.

At the beginning of this chapter we wrote that 'the archosaurs were mere reptiles and should therefore have been greatly inferior to the contemporary mammals!' But there were no mammals in the Triassic, only mammal-like reptiles, far more primitive than the mammals of today. And, conversely, we have seen that some of the Triassic archosaurs, although classified as reptiles, appear to have been far more advanced in their skeletal structures than are modern reptiles – more highly evolved, even, than present-day archosaurs (represented only by the crocodiles). They may also have been more advanced in other, mainly physiological characters, but of that we cannot be certain. (All this emphasizes the fact that the animals of long ago, when assigned to a class which is still living at the present time, cannot be assumed automatically to have possessed all the class characters of the living members.) In the light of these circumstances it should no longer seem paradoxical that the archosaurian reptiles achieved domination over the mammal-like reptiles of the day and maintained it for 140 million years.

12· Theropod dinosaurs: the carnivorous bipeds

Coelophysis, a coelurosaur from the Upper Trias of New Mexico. Typical length 2.5 metres.

Right. Compsognathus, a very small coelurosaur from the Upper Jurassic of southern Germany. Length about 65 centimetres. Its neck is bent right round so that its head is upside down above its back.

At last, after what may have seemed like endless preliminaries, we have reached the point in this book where we can begin the straightforward description of the different sorts of dinosaur. Obviously we shall not describe every one of the hundreds of named species; even an account of every genus would be as boring for the reader as it would be for the author. We shall try, however, to give brief portrayals of all the major types – the newly discovered as well as the more familiar; those that are not so described may safely be regarded as nothing more than 'variations on a theme'. And we shall begin with the theropods.

We explained in Chapter 10 that the saurischian dinosaurs are classified into two suborders – the Theropoda and the Sauropodomorpha. The theropods are a very distinctive group; they were all habitual or even obligatory bipeds, and, with a few notable exceptions (see below), they were all exclusively carnivores. They are generally subdivided – conveniently but probably incorrectly – into the small, lightly built coelurosaurs and the very much larger, more heavily built carnosaurs; we shall here adopt a more recent classification and distinguish a third group of intermediate size range, the fast-moving and highly predacious deinonychosaurs.

The coelurosaurs

The first coelurosaurs were among the earliest of all dinosaurs, living in Late Triassic times.

One of the best known is a little animal called *Coelophysis* ('hollow form'), of which many well-preserved skeletons were found at Ghost Ranch in New Mexico; they were of all sizes, from newly hatched (or newly born) babies to fully grown adults. Even the adults, however, were only about 2.5 metres long and 1 metre tall, and were so lightly built that they probably weighed no more than 20 kilogrammes. The head was long and pointed; the teeth were sharp, with fine saw-toothed edges like steak-knives; the neck, body, tail and hind legs were all long and slender. The feet were bird-like, with only three toes touching the ground. The fore-limbs were shorter, with four-fingered hands which could probably be used for grasping.

Altogether *Coelophysis* seems to have been a highly active little predator with an insatiable appetite; it is likely that it chased anything that moved, grabbing it with its hands and snapping at it with its jaws. Incidentally, a couple of well-preserved adult skeletons have been found, each with the remains of tiny *Coelophysis* skeletons inside it. This might be a case of live birth – or, less pleasantly, it could suggest cannibalism.

Dinosaurs like *Coelophysis* – some rather bigger, others even smaller – seem to have continued throughout the whole of the Jurassic and Cretaceous. One very small coelurosaur is *Compsognathus* ('pretty jaw') from the Upper Jurassic of southern Germany. It was one of the smallest of all dinosaurs, with a total length of

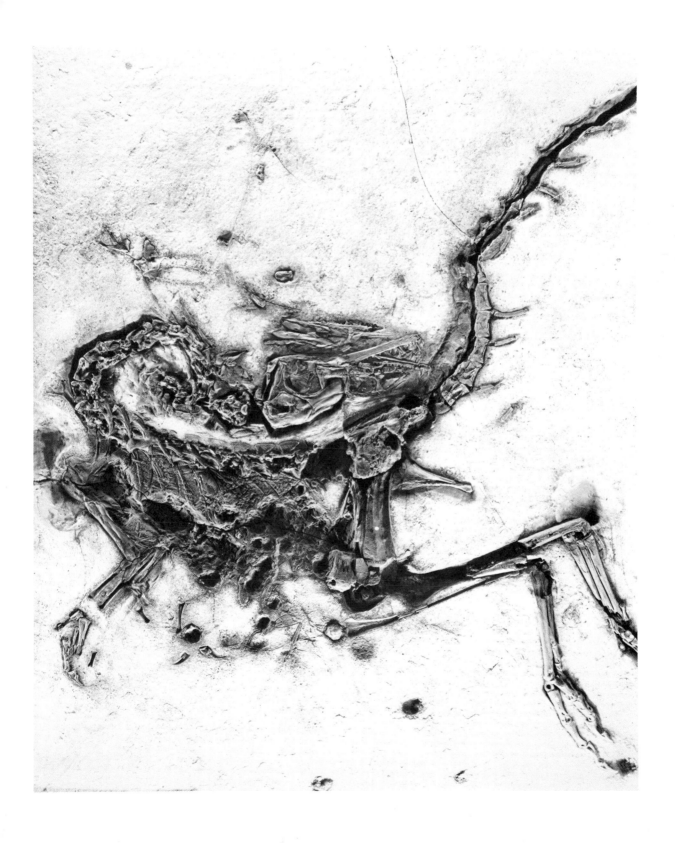

Deinonychus, a deinonychosaur from the Lower Cretaceous of Montana. Typical length 2.7 metres.

60 or 70 centimetres – no bigger than a domestic chicken; it should be borne in mind, however, that the only known specimen might well have been a juvenile, not yet fully grown.

A 'specialized' type of theropod which has been known for many years is the so-called ostrich dinosaur, *Ornithomimus* ('bird imitator,; *see* Plate 18), found fairly widely in the Cretaceous rocks of North America and Asia. Ornithomimids were coelurosaurs which had grown quite large, with a length of 4 metres or even more. The neck was long, the head was comparatively tiny, and there were no teeth in the beak-like jaws; indeed, at first glance a

reconstruction of the animal does have an ostrich-like appearance, but of course an ostrich – unlike *Ornithomimus* – does not have a long tail. The fore-limbs were longer than in other coelurosaurs, and the three-fingered hands were probably used for grasping, pulling and tearing (another difference from the ostrich, which has small feathered wings). *Ornithomimus* may have lived on a diet of small animals, insects, eggs and fruit.

The deinonychosaurs
Deinonychosaurs are known only from Cretaceous rocks so must presumably have evolved

Ornithomimus, an ostrich dinosaur from the Cretaceous of North America and Asia. Typical length 4.2 metres.

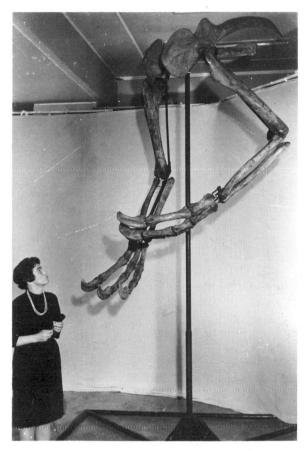

The shoulder-bones and fore-limbs (nothing else is known) of the strange theropod dinosaur *Deinocheirus*, with Professor Zofia Kielan-Jaworowska

stretched its tail back horizontally when running and used it for balance.

Another new theropod find is even more exciting than the discovery of *Deinonychus* – perhaps all the more so because there is only one specimen, and that is far from complete. It was unearthed in 1965, in the Upper Cretaceous rocks of the Gobi Desert in Mongolia. All that was found was the shoulder-bones and fore-limbs of a large theropod with a three-fingered, grasping hand – perhaps another ostrich dinosaur. But what is so remarkable about it is its enormous size; the fore-limb alone was about 2.4 metres long! One shudders to think of the size of the entire animal, as yet unknown. For obvious reasons this creature has been named *Deinocheirus*, 'terrible hand'; its classification is uncertain.

The carnosaurs

Now we must turn our attention to the carnosaurs, which make their first appearance in the fossil record rather later than did the coelurosaurs. Indeed, they may have evolved from them. One of the earliest carnosaurs was *Megalosaurus* ('big lizard'; *see* Plate 3), which lived in England and France throughout the whole of the Jurassic period and into the earlier part of the Cretaceous. It might best be described as an enormously bigger, more heavily built *Coelophysis* in which the head had been enlarged even more than the rest of the animal but the neck had been shortened and the fore-limbs had shrunk. The entire creature was over 6 metres long and 3 metres tall when erect, weighing about 2 tonnes. Historically *Megalosaurus* is very important because the first recorded dinosaur bone (1676) probably belonged to it; moreover, as already mentioned in an earlier chapter, it was the first dinosaur to be named, the first to be described (1824) and one of the three forming the group which Owen named 'Dinosauria' in 1841. (It is also one of the dinosaurs modelled in concrete in the grounds of the Crystal Palace – *see* p.52.) Unfortunately most *Megalosaurus* specimens are far from complete, but the animal has left us many examples of its footprints – even whole trackways – in the rocks of southern England.

from coelurosaurian forbears. The best-known genus is *Deinonychus* itself (Plate 19), discovered as recently as 1964 in the Lower Cretaceous of Montana, U.S.A.; that is why there is no mention of it in the older dinosaur books. It was a lightly built, fast-running theropod about 2.5 or 3 metres long, with a fairly large head and a grasping hand. But it possessed two remarkable features. First, the second toe of the four on the hind foot did not reach the ground; it ended in an enormous claw, shaped like a sickle, which, kicked backwards, would inflict a fearsome wound upon an enemy (hence the name, which means 'terrible claw'). Secondly, the long tail was strengthened by bundles of bony rods which, so it seems, must have locked it almost rigid when pulled tight; the reptile probably

Dilophosaurus, a carnosaur from the Lower Jurassic of Arizona. Typical length 6 metres.

Spinosaurus, a 'sail-backed' carnosaur from the Upper Cretaceous of Egypt

Allosaurus, a carnosaur from the Upper Jurassic of the western U.S.A. Typical length 10 metres.

The Upper Jurassic strata of western North America contain many skeletons of a close relative of *Megalosaurus*, the even larger *Allosaurus* ('different lizard'). This carnosaur, 10 metres long and nearly 4 metres tall, was the great hunter of its day, preying upon the gigantic sauropods (like *Brontosaurus* and *Diplodocus*) that we shall discuss in the next chapter.

Other relatives of *Megalosaurus* had little peculiarities. *Dilophosaurus* ('two-ridged lizard'; *see* Plate 12) from the Lower Jurassic of Arizona, first found in 1954 by a Navajo Indian and more than 6 metres long, had two high crests running along the top of its head. These crests, though paper-thin in places, were strengthened by heavier struts of bone; perhaps they were of use in distinguishing males from females. *Ceratosaurus* ('horn lizard'; *see* Plate 2) from the Upper Jurassic of the western U.S.A. was somewhat smaller than *Megalosaurus* itself; its special features were a little horn on top of its snout and a bony knob above

Tarbosaurus, a carnosaur very similar to *Tyrannosaurus*, from the Upper Cretaceous of Mongolia. Typical length 12 metres

each eye. The gigantic *Spinosaurus* from the Upper Cretaceous of Egypt had enormously long neural spines on the vertebrae of its back, up to 1.8 metres long; they presumably supported a 'sail' which functioned as a heat exchanger (just like that of the fin-backed pelycosaur *Dimetrodon*, depicted on p.10). Isolated vertebrae of the same type suggest that similar carnosaurs lived elsewhere at other times; for example, the Wealden (Lower Cretaceous) of England has yielded a few of these, to which the name *Altispinax* has been given (*see* Plate 5).

In the Late Cretaceous, just before the end of the Age of Dinosaurs, the carnosaurs became bigger still. Biggest of all was the famous *Tyrannosaurus* ('tyrant lizard'; *see* Plate 18) of western North America and Mongolia, generally believed to be 'the largest flesh-eating animal that ever walked the earth'. This terrifying creature was 12 metres long, 5 metres tall and weighed about 7 tonnes; the head alone measured 1.25 metres and the saw-edged teeth reached a length of 15 centimetres. The forelimbs, however, were tiny, with only two fingers on each hand; it seems unlikely that they could have been of any use to the animal. But this would not have mattered. *Tyrannosaurus* probably gripped and tore its prey, like a hawk or an owl, with the great clawed feet on its enormous, immensely powerful hind legs. Small wonder that the plant-eating dinosaur *Triceratops*, found in great numbers in the same deposits, needed horns as weapons and a neck frill for defence.

Highly successful though *Tyrannosaurus* may have been in its day, it nevertheless disappeared without trace 65 million years ago, at the end of the Cretaceous period. Its final extinction (and that of its contemporaries) rang down the curtain on the last scene of the dinosaur story. The stage was then set for the great radiation of the Tertiary mammals and the eventual evolution of man.

13 · Sauropodomorph dinosaurs: *Diplodocus* and its relatives

The sauropodomorphs were very different animals from the theropods, even though both groups are classified together as saurischians. Indeed, as already mentioned (p.87), it is not impossible that the Sauropodomorpha and the Theropoda evolved separately from the Thecodontia; if they did, then the order 'Saurischia' would be an artificial assemblage.

The two subdivisions of the Sauropodomorpha are the gigantic, quadrupedal, herbivorous Sauropoda and the smaller, partly bipedal, partly carnivorous Prosauropoda. The prosauropods preceded the sauropods in time; the sauropods are the more important, however, and will therefore be considered first.

The sauropods

In most respects nearly all the sauropods were more or less alike. An enormous body tapered forwards into a remarkably long neck and backwards into an even longer tail. The neck ended in a ridiculously small head with the nostrils on top. The jaws do not seem to have been very strong; they bore weak teeth shaped like pegs or spoons, suitable only for feeding on soft vegetation. The tail was thick and strong at the base but slender and whip-like towards its end; the animal may well have used it as a whip with which to lash its enemies, just like some modern lizards, for it had no other means of self-defence. The legs were long, straight and pillar-like, with short-toed feet, altogether rather like an elephant's; the back legs, in most cases, were much longer than the front. These animals have been found throughout the whole of the Jurassic and Cretaceous systems, but, as yet, have not been reported from the earliest rocks of the Age of Dinosaurs (Upper Trias).

It might have been expected that the first sauropods would be comparatively small and that they would get larger as time went by; thus the Late Jurassic forms would be bigger than the Early and Middle Jurassic, and the Cretaceous ones bigger still. The facts, however, are demonstrably different; it is the sauropods of the Late Jurassic that are the most numerous, the most varied, and the biggest of all.

Let us take a closer look at just a few of these. A very typical and well known sauropod is *Brontosaurus*, the 'thunder lizard' (more properly called *Apatosaurus*, the 'deceit lizard'; *see* Plate 18). This Late Jurassic dinosaur from the western U.S.A. was 20 metres long, 4.5 metres tall at the shoulder, and weighed about 30 tonnes. In the same deposits as *Apatosaurus* we find *Diplodocus* ('double beam'). This famous animal was generally similar to *Apatosaurus* but was longer and more slender, indeed it was probably one of the longest of all dinosaurs (26 metres); its weight, on the other hand, has been estimated at only 10 tonnes.

An English sauropod of the same general form is *Cetiosauriscus* (similar in some respects to *Cetiosaurus*, 'whale lizard', the first sauropod to be discovered). This is found a little lower in the Upper Jurassic and was somewhat smaller, no more than 15 metres long. Its remains are usually much scrappier than the well-preserved, nearly complete skeletons of its American relatives, but a fairly good skeleton – the best so far – was dug out near Stamford (Lincolnshire) in 1968.

Rather different from all these was *Brachiosaurus* ('arm lizard'; *see* Plate 2) from the Late Jurassic of the western U.S.A. and of Tanzania. In this animal it was the front legs which were the longer, not the hind as in nearly all other dinosaurs; because of this its back sloped steeply upwards towards its vertical neck. Until a few years ago *Brachiosaurus* was thought to be the largest land animal that had ever lived; the head was 12.6 metres from the ground (tall enough to peer over the top of a four-storey building!), the bone of the upper arm alone is over 2.1 metres long, and the creature's live weight has been estimated at 80 tonnes (20 times as heavy as a large elephant). Only one museum in the world has a mounted skeleton of this enormous beast – the Natural Science Museum in East Berlin (*see* photograph opposite).

The largest mounted dinosaur skeleton in the world,
Brachiosaurus from the Upper Jurassic of Tanzania,
standing about 12.6 metres high in the East Berlin
Natural Science Museum

Cetiosauriscus, a sauropod from the Upper Jurassic of England. Typical length 15 metres.

In 1972, however, some bones of a new sauropod dinosaur, even bigger than *Brachiosaurus*, were found in Colorado. One vertebra alone was about 1.5 metres long! This animal, as yet unnamed (*Reader's Digest* has referred to it unofficially as '*Supersaurus*') is thought to have been more than 15 metres tall and as much as 30 metres in length. It must have weighed a great deal more than the 80 tonnes of *Brachiosaurus*.

This largest dinosaur known to man – in fact, the largest animal of any sort, at least on land – is in striking contrast to another dinosaur found very recently (1977) in Argentina, in beds of latest Triassic or earliest Jurassic age. The new discovery, described from several specimens as *Mussaurus*, was no bigger than a thrush; the skeleton bears some resemblance to that of a prosauropod (*see* p.114), but the tiny skull is remarkably sauropod-like. The proportions of the skull suggest that it was probably a juvenile. Close to the skeletons, almost perfect, were found two small eggs.

Until very recently most dinosaur experts believed that these great animals spent much of their time (if not all of it) in shallow water – in swamps and around the edges of lakes – feeding on the soft water-plants. That is how they are described in most books on the subject, and the pictures in the books show the same sort of thing. First, it was said that their legs were not strong enough to support their vast bodies on land and that they needed the buoyancy of the water to hold them up. Secondly, it was also believed that their weak teeth could deal only with soft water-weed. Finally, it was thought that the position of the external nasal openings on top of the head was a special feature which enabled the animals to breathe while almost completely under water (perhaps in hiding from their enemies, such as *Allosaurus*). But this belief is no longer held by everybody. Indeed, there are many reasons for believing that the sauropods were proper land-dwellers. Because the external nasal openings are on top of the skull it does not necessarily follow that the actual nostrils were on top of the head and that the animal lived in water; there are some present-day animals (like elephants and tapirs) in which the external nasal openings are on top of the skull, but we know that the nostrils are in fact at the end of a proboscis or trunk, and some sauropods may well have possessed a similar structure. Animals that live in the water (like crocodiles) usually have an entirely different arrangement, with their nostrils at the end of a long snout. Again, the teeth of sauropods were not as weak as is usually believed and are often very worn, suggesting that the animals' food was something rather harder than water-weed.

Other observations, too, agree with the idea of a life on land, with only occasional excursions into the water. For example, the shape of the body is not suited to an aquatic existence. Reptiles and mammals living in water usually have barrel-shaped bodies with short necks, tails flattened for swimming and short legs (sometimes paddle-like). As we have seen, however, the sauropods had deep bodies, long necks – perhaps for feeding on the leaves of high trees – whip-like tails and long, straight, elephant-

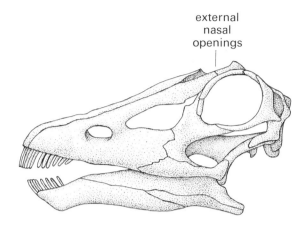

external
nasal
openings

The skull of *Diplodocus*, showing the position of the external nasal openings and the characteristic teeth. Length of skull 65 centimetres.

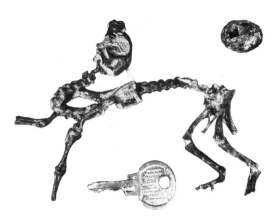

The skeleton of the smallest dinosaur known, *Mussaurus*, from near the Triassic-Jurassic boundary in Argentina. Skull length 32 millimetres. The egg was found only a few centimetres away; its longest axis measures 25 millimetres.

Excavating on the '*Supersaurus*' site in Colorado. The gigantic bone longer than the man lying next to it is a shoulder-blade.

like legs. The sauropod skeleton is designed in such a way as to make it as light as possible, yet extremely strong to carry the animal's enormous weight. Sauropod feet are *not* wide and spreading, as is usual in animals that walk on soft mud or loose sand; on the contrary, they are (for the size of the animal) small and compact, so that if the creature had walked out on to the swamp it would have got hopelessly bogged down. Finally, the nature of the sediments in which sauropods are usually buried does not suggest a swampy environment, and the other fossils found with them are chiefly the remains of plants and animals that lived on land.

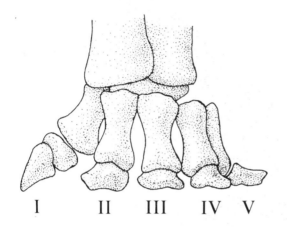

I   II   III   IV V

The front foot of *Apatosaurus*

However, the most powerful argument against a fully aquatic existence for the sauropods may be this. If the sauropod's body had been deep in the water, the weight of the water pressing on its chest and lungs would almost certainly have prevented it from breathing in.

One idea that seems to have become very popular is the belief that a dinosaur – more particularly a sauropod dinosaur – possessed two brains, one in its head and the other in its hip region. This belief is based on the fact that a sauropod – like all backboned animals – had a swelling of its spinal nerve cord just above its back legs. Now the sauropod happens to have had a tiny head and enormous hips; this means that the swelling in the hips (which, in most other animals, is much smaller than the brain)

was here the larger of the two. But that is no reason to suppose that the swelling in the hips was capable of 'thinking'; as in other backboned animals, including ourselves, it was mainly concerned with automatic control of the hind legs. In any case, the swelling of the nerve cord may not have been nearly as big as is generally believed; the enlarged cavity inside the vertebrae need not have been completely filled with nervous tissue, for in some living animals a large part of it is occupied by a glycogen store.

Incidentally, recent discoveries have shown that some Late Cretaceous sauropods possessed a few protective bony plates embedded in the skin.

Although of such gigantic size, the sauropods did not produce gigantic eggs to match. If they had done so, the shell would have been so thick that neither could enough air have passed through it to supply the baby dinosaur inside, nor could the baby dinosaur, when ready to hatch, have succeeded in breaking out. What we know of sauropod eggs is based upon abundant finds of bits of egg-shell, occasionally of whole eggs, and sometimes even of complete clutches (most often consisting of five eggs) in the South of France. These eggs are roundish-oval in shape, with the longest axis about 25 centimetres in length and with a rough outer surface covered in small bumps. The only animal whose remains are found in the same strata and which was big enough to have produced such eggs is a sauropod called *Hypselosaurus* – 'high lizard'.

The prosauropods

Finally, having dealt with the sauropods, we must turn very briefly to the other sauropodomorphs – the prosauropods. These reptiles lived only at the beginning of the Age of Dinosaurs, in Late Triassic times and Early Jurassic. They were vaguely sauropod-like in general build, but they were smaller, sometimes much smaller (only a couple of metres long); as mentioned above, some may well have been occasional bipeds and some may have been carnivores or omnivores rather than vegetarians. *Plateosaurus* ('flat lizard'; *see* Plate 1) from southern Germany is a well-known prosauropod; it was about 6 metres long and rather clumsy in appearance. The small head, with flattened teeth, was supported by a neck much shorter than that of a proper sauropod. Of similar dimensions was *Riojasaurus* from Argentina; smaller prosauropods occur in South Africa and Basutoland (*Massospondylus*) and in the eastern U.S.A. (*Anchisaurus*).

It used to be thought that the prosauropods of the Late Triassic, as their name suggests, evolved into the true sauropods of the Jurassic immediately following. They had only to grow bigger, to go back to walking on all fours *all* the time and to change their proportions a little. But many authorities no longer believe this, preferring (for various reasons) to regard the prosauropods as 'great-uncles' of the sauropods rather than as 'grandfathers' – in other words, as a side-branch of the sauropod family tree which died out at the end of the Triassic. The Triassic ancestors of the largest beasts that ever trod the earth have yet to be discovered.

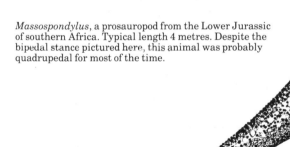

Massospondylus, a prosauropod from the Lower Jurassic of southern Africa. Typical length 4 metres. Despite the bipedal stance pictured here, this animal was probably quadrupedal for most of the time.

14 · Ornithopod dinosaurs: herbivorous bipeds

The Ornithopoda, we recall, were one of the four suborders of the Ornithischia (the 'bird-hipped' dinosaurs) and the only one of the four in which the members showed some tendency towards bipedality.

The 'ordinary' ornithopods were a long-lived group, making their first appearance in the Early Jurassic and surviving right through to the end of the Cretaceous. They were also remarkable in that, by and large, they were not very different from one another (except in size). From them evolved three rather specialized groups of ornithopods. One, the hadrosaurs or duck-billed dinosaurs, was enormously abundant in Late Cretaceous times. The other two were both very rare; they were the psittacosaurs or parrot dinosaurs of the Early Cretaceous and the pachycephalosaurs or dome-headed dinosaurs of both Early and Late Cretaceous. It is now thought by some, however, that the dome-headed dinosaurs should not be regarded as ornithopods at all but should be placed in a group of their own.

Not many ornithopods have been found in the Lower Jurassic; indeed, until the early nineteen-sixties only one ornithischian dinosaur (the armoured *Scelidosaurus*) and a few scraps were known from Lower Jurassic strata, whereas saurischians are already abundant in Upper Triassic beds. In 1962, however, a remarkable little ornithopod skull no bigger than a rabbit's was found in the Lower Jurassic of South Africa; we (the author and his friend who discovered it) named it *Heterodontosaurus*, the 'different-toothed lizard' (*see* Plate 14). As the name suggests, the most unusual thing about *Heterodontosaurus* was its teeth. In the front of the upper jaw were small simple teeth which bit against a horny toothless beak on the lower jaw and were presumably used for nipping off the leaves on which it fed. In the back of both jaws was a row of tall teeth, very close together, which had worn each other down to form one long flat biting surface; their inner and outer surfaces were ridged and grooved and they worked like the blades of a

pair of scissors, cutting up the food as it passed between them from the mouth into the cheeks. The muscular cheeks then pushed the food back into the mouth so that it could be swallowed or, if necessary, passed between the teeth again to be chopped even finer. Most remarkable of all, between the front teeth and the back teeth in the upper jaw, and between the beak and the back teeth in the lower jaw, was a much bigger tooth or small tusk – rather like the canine tooth ('eye-tooth') of a dog. What this was used for we do not know; the male dinosaurs may have used it for fighting among themselves.

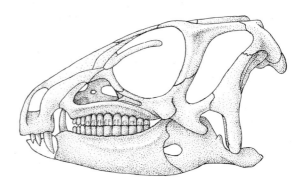

The skull of *Heterodontosaurus*, an ornithopod from the Lower Jurassic of southern Africa. Length of skull 9 centimetres.

Since the *Heterodontosaurus* skull was described, an almost complete skeleton of the same genus has been found. This shows it to have been a lightly built, fast-running, bipedal animal.

Living also in southern Africa at about the same time as *Heterodontosaurus* – perhaps even a little earlier – was another small ornithopod called *Lesothosaurus* (named after the country of its discovery; *see* Plate 11). This dinosaur, one of the few well-known Early Jurassic ornithopods, was generally similar to *Heterodontosaurus* but had a simpler, more primitive skull and teeth. The skull was flatter; there were no 'canine' teeth; and the back teeth were not placed close together or

Heterodontosaurus restored. Estimated length of whole animal 90 centimetres.

Lesothosaurus, a more primitive ornithopod from the Lower Jurassic of southern Africa. Typical length 90 centimetres.

worn down to form one long biting surface but were separate and shaped like leaves with crenulate edges. It also seems that there were no muscular cheeks.

By Late Jurassic and Early Cretaceous times the ornithopods had become very numerous; one of the most famous is the familiar *Iguanodon* (*see* Plate 5). We have already met *Iguanodon* in Chapter 6 and read the story of how Mrs Mantell found its teeth in Sussex in 1822, of how Dr Mantell reconstructed it wrongly as a quadruped with one of its spiky thumb-bones on top of its snout like a horn, of how a concrete restoration of the animal was completed at the Crystal Palace in 1854, and of how the magnificent skeletons found in Belgium in 1877–78 showed us what it was really like. *Iguanodon* was also the second dinosaur to be named and described (1825) and, together with *Megalosaurus* and *Hylaeosaurus*, formed the little group which Owen later named 'Dinosauria' (1841).

Iguanodon lived throughout the whole of the Early Cretaceous, from 140 to about 105 million years ago, and its bones have been found in Germany, Rumania and North Africa as well as in southern England and Belgium. There are also footprints and trackways (especially near Swanage in Dorset, England) which are supposed to have been made by this animal. *Iguanodon* was appreciably bigger than the flesh-eating *Megalosaurus* found in the same deposits, for it was over 9 metres long, 5 metres tall when standing upright and must have weighed about $4\frac{1}{2}$ tonnes. Although, in general, its footprints suggest that it walked only on its hind legs, it must also have walked quadrupedally at times because it has hooves rather than claws on its front feet (or 'hands') as well as on its hind feet. Only the thumb has the big spiky claw sticking out sideways; the animal probably used this to defend itself against its enemies.

Tenontosaurus, an ornithopod from the Lower Cretaceous of Montana. Typical length 6.5 metres.

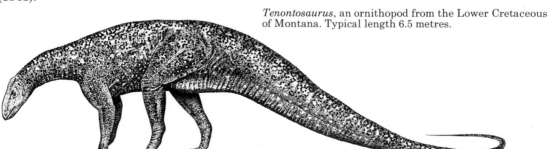

Hypsilophodon, an ornithopod from the Lower Cretaceous of the Isle of Wight. Typical length 1.5 metres.

Edmontosaurus, a duck-billed dinosaur from the Upper Cretaceous of western Canada. Typical length 13 metres.

Another well-known English ornithopod is *Hypsilophodon* ('high ridge tooth'; *see* Plate 5), which is like a very much smaller and lightly built *Iguanodon*; indeed, it was never much longer than 1.5 metres, half of that being tail, and its weight was measured in kilogrammes rather than in tonnes. Because it was so small and light it probably stood and walked on two legs more often than did its much bigger relation; it used to be thought that it lived in the trees, but that is no longer believed. *Hypsilophodon* too is of Early Cretaceous age, about 115 million years old; oddly enough, all the specimens known (about twenty or so) come from one particular place called Cowleaze Chine on the south-west coast of the Isle of Wight. Among the more noticeable differences from *Iguanodon* are the presence of a few small teeth in the front of the upper jaw (lost in most ornithopods) and the lack of a thumb spike.

The hadrosaurs or duck-billed dinosaurs

A very important group of ornithopods, rather different from the 'ordinary' ones like *Iguanodon*, were the hadrosaurs or duck-billed dinosaurs. A typical hadrosaur was *Anatosaurus* ('duck lizard'; *see* Plate 18) from the Upper Cretaceous of western North America. This reptile was about 9 metres long and 4 metres tall and it weighed some 3 tonnes. In general shape it was much like an *Iguanodon* with a long narrow head and a duck-like bill. There were no teeth in the front of the jaws, but at the back there were many hundreds of grinding teeth arranged in a very complicated manner to form what is called a dental battery; the teeth were being worn down all the time and new ones were always growing up to replace them, so it is obvious that the dinosaur was eating something rather hard and coarse.

Hadrosaurs, again like *Iguanodon*, probably walked on all fours for much of the time. There

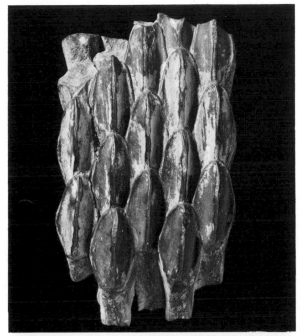

was a strong tail, flattened from side to side and broad from top to bottom; this would be very useful when swimming to drive the animal through the water. The fingers of the hand were webbed, which again suggests that they lived in the water. In fact, it has generally been believed that the duck-billed dinosaurs *did* live largely in lakes and swamps (they certainly took to the water for safety from such terrible flesh-eaters as *Tyrannosaurus*) but within the last few years doubts have been cast on this. Remarkably, a couple of duckbills have been found in a mummified condition (*see* p. 71), with a clear impression of the skin on the surrounding rock and with the contents of the stomach still well enough preserved for us to be able to tell what the animal had been eating (quantities of pine needles, together with the twigs, seeds and fruits of other land plants).

There were many sorts of hadrosaur, all built on the same basic plan but differing in detail. The most noticeable difference lay in the fact that some of them had strange crests on top of their heads, while others (like *Anatosaurus*) did not. The crests themselves were of many dif-

Corythosaurus, a crested duckbill from the Upper Cretaceous of western Canada. Typical length 9 metres.

Part of a tooth battery of a duck-billed dinosaur, *Trachodon*, from the Upper Cretaceous of Wyoming. Width of specimen as preserved 4.2 centimetres.
Above. Outer view.
Below. Inner view. The composite nature of the battery, with overlapping teeth, is clearly visible on the left.

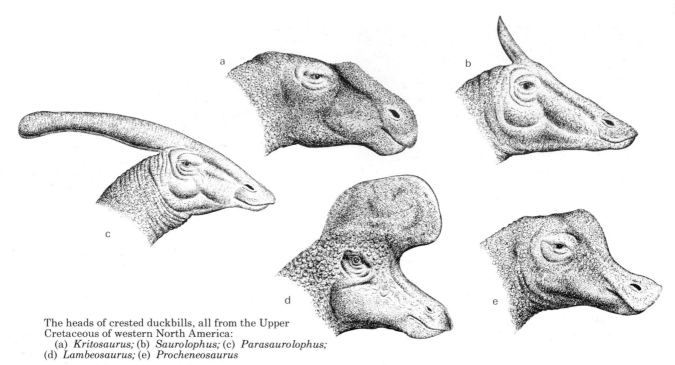

The heads of crested duckbills, all from the Upper
Cretaceous of western North America:
(a) *Kritosaurus;* (b) *Saurolophus;* (c) *Parasaurolophus;*
(d) *Lambeosaurus;* (e) *Procheneosaurus*

ferent shapes (*see* figures above); some were
solid, but most of them were hollow. For example, *Corythosaurus* ('helmet lizard'; *see* Plate
8), which was rather bigger than *Anatosaurus*
and weighed nearly 4 tonnes, had a hollow
helmet-like crest covering the entire top of the
skull. The question of what these crests were for
has never been answered with certainty, although many ideas have been put forward.
Some ideas are rather unlikely; among them we
may include 'snorkelling', storing air for breathing under water, preventing water or sand
from getting into the lungs, serving as the base
for a proboscis, and providing attachments for
ligaments and muscles which supported and
moved the heavy head. Better suggestions are
that they were used for improving the sense of
smell or in social behaviour, especially mating.
This latter category would include their use as
sound resonators (perhaps they made some sort
of trumpeting noise) and as characteristic vi-
sual signs by which the animals could recognize
others of their own species, determine to which
sex they belonged or their position in the
'pecking order' and display to them accordingly; it would also include their use by rival
males as weapons and as shields in butting and
fighting each other.

Evolutionary trends towards the hadrosaurs
are suggested by an interesting variation on the
Iguanodon theme, discovered in 1965. A veritable 'dinosaur cemetery' was located in the
upper part of the Lower Cretaceous beds of the
southern Sahara, in the African republic of
Niger; and from that 'cemetery' palaeontologists secured two complete skeletons – together with partial remains of other individuals
– of a slender, altogether new iguanodontid
which they named *Ouranosaurus* ('valiant mon-
itor lizard'). This animal is characterized by
extremely long neural spines on the vertebrae
of the trunk and tail (which would have formed
a high ridge down the middle of its back
and might possibly have supported a heat-
exchanging 'sail') and it already possessed several hadrosaur-like characters of the skull,
including a muzzle like a duck's bill. *Ouranosaurus* probably lay close to the origins of the
hadrosaurs.

The psittacosaurs or parrot dinosaurs
Finally we shall mention two very rare groups
of ornithopods, the psittacosaurs or parrot
dinosaurs and the pachycephalosaurs or dome-

heads. *Psittacosaurus* ('parrot lizard'; *see* Plate 13) was one of the former; it is found in the Lower Cretaceous (about 110 million years old) of Mongolia and China. This little animal, only 1.5–2.5 metres long, had a deep narrow skull and a powerful parrot-like beak. It was obviously a biped and used its hands for grasping. There is evidence which suggests that the psittacosaurs lay close to the evolutionary line running from the ornithopods to the ceratopians (the horned dinosaurs, to be described in the next chapter); indeed, some would prefer to classify the psittacosaurs within the Ceratopia rather than within the Ornithopoda. But the evidence for such a relationship, although reasonable, is not conclusive. It is interesting to note that, if the horned dinosaurs *are* descended from something closely related to the psittacosaurs and if that ancestor too was bipedal, then the horned dinosaurs must have *reverted* to a quadrupedal stance and gait – in other words, they must have been secondary quadrupeds.

The pachycephalosaurs or domeheads

Altogether very different was *Pachycephalosaurus* ('thick-headed lizard'; *see* Plate 18), one of the dome-headed dinosaurs. This is from the Upper Cretaceous of the U.S.A., but there are related forms in Mongolia, Madagascar, and in the Lower Cretaceous of the Isle of Wight in England. *Pachycephalosaurus* was a large bipedal ornithischian, the skull alone being 60 centimetres long. The skull roof is enormously thickened, with a rough and bumpy surface; it has been suggested that here too the males butted each other with their heads in the mating season, rather like male sheep and goats today. As stated at the beginning of this chapter, it may be that the pachycephalosaurs are not ornithopods at all but should constitute an entirely independent suborder of bipedal ornithischians.

All in all, it seems not unreasonable to regard the ornithopods as filling the same place in nature a hundred million years or so ago as do the hoofed mammals in our modern world, especially as many of them – like the hoofed mammals – seem to have lived in herds and fed on the abundant vegetation. This is also true of the other ornithischians that we shall meet in the next chapter.

Ouranosaurus, a 'sail-backed' ornithopod from the Lower Cretaceous of Niger. Typical length 7 metres.

Psittacosaurus, a parrot dinosaur from the Lower Cretaceous of Mongolia. Typical length 2 metres.

Stegoceras, a dome-headed dinosaur from the Upper Cretaceous of Alberta

15 · Horned, plated and armoured dinosaurs

These three groups of ornithischian dinosaurs shared one common characteristic which distinguished them from the fourth group, the ornithopods: all their members were entirely quadrupedal. If that is a primitive character, however – and we happen to think that it is, certainly in the plated and armoured dinosaurs and possibly in the horned – then it cannot be used as evidence of a relationship between those three groups closer than exists between any of them and the ornithopods. Indeed, it is generally believed that the three groups dealt with in this chapter are related only in so far as they are certainly all ornithischians, and we deal with them together only for the sake of convenience.

The ceratopians or horned dinosaurs

Let us begin with the best known of the horned dinosaurs or Ceratopia, the familiar *Triceratops* ('three-horned face'; *see* Plate 2). This animal was extremely common in western North America towards the end of Late Cretaceous times, 70–65 million years ago. We may picture vast herds of these great rhinoceros-like animals, 7 metres long and weighing from 8 to 9 tonnes, roaming the plains and grazing the abundant vegetation. The head was enormous, for the skull alone was more than 2 metres long. At the front was a beak, behind it a set of shearing teeth; on top of the snout was a short thick nose-horn; above the eyes, pointing forwards, was a pair of sharp brow-horns 1 metre long; and, from the back of the skull, a great solid frill projected backwards over the neck and shoulders. The legs were thick and strong, with little hooves instead of sharp claws, and there was a short but heavy tail. The whole of the body was protected by a leathery skin. Although a plant-eater, this dinosaur was well able to look after itself; even a hungry *Tyrannosaurus* (which lived in the same region at the same time) would think twice before braving those vicious horns. It seems that the male *Triceratops* also fought each other (probably in the mating season) because their neck frills often show the marks of wounds produced in such battles.

Many other ceratopians lived in North America in Late Cretaceous times. They differed from each other mainly in the pattern of the horns and the shape of the neck frill. *Pentaceratops* ('five-horned face') had two more horns than *Triceratops*, the extra two projecting sideways from the cheek region. *Monoclonius* ('single shoot') had a very long horn on its snout, two small brow-lumps, and a short frill with a large

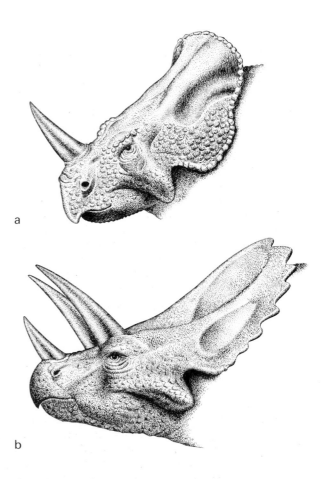

a

b

The heads of horned dinosaurs, both from the Upper Cretaceous of western North America: (a) *Monoclonius*; (b) *Pentaceratops*

hole on each side. *Styracosaurus* ('spike lizard') also had a long nose-horn; but it had practically no brow-horns and the frill was decorated with six long backwardly pointing spikes, the last two being the longest (*see* p. 13). *Chasmosaurus* ('chasm lizard') had a small nose-horn, fairly large brow-horns, and a long frill with very large holes through the bone. Rather different from all these was *Pachyrhinosaurus* ('thick-nosed lizard'); this large dinosaur (*see* Plate 10) had no horns at all but instead, covering the top of the skull between the nose and the eyes, there was a great thick plate of bone hollowed out above like a crater.

Now let us go backwards in time, from 70 to 90 million years ago (still in the Late Cretaceous). Horned dinosaurs were then only just beginning, not in North America but in what is now the Gobi Desert of Mongolia, and they were so primitive that the only trace of a horn was a mere bump on top of the snout. The animal in question was *Protoceratops* ('first horned face'); it was only about 2 metres long (*see* Plate 9) and weighed no more than 180 kilogrammes, very small for a horned dinosaur. The skull was relatively enormous, deep and narrow with a parrot-like beak; as in later ceratopians, it was extended backwards into a curved bony neck frill which not only protected the neck and shoulders but was also used for the attachment of the powerful jaw and neck muscles. The body was short and squat.

Chasmosaurus, a horned dinosaur from the Upper Cretaceous of western North America

Pachyrhinosaurus, a hornless ceratopian from the Upper Cretaceous of Alberta

Protoceratops, a primitive ceratopian from the Upper Cretaceous of Mongolia. Typical length 2 metres.

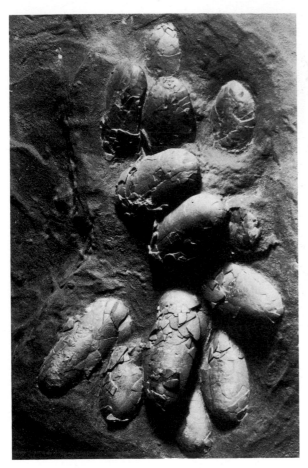

A 'nest' of *Protoceratops* eggs, from the Gobi Desert of Mongolia. Each egg is up to 20 centimetres long.

Right. Stegosaurus, a plated dinosaur from the Upper Jurassic of the western U.S.A. Typical length 6 metres.

Protoceratops is a very common dinosaur; perhaps the most interesting and unusual thing about it is that it is known in various growth stages – eggs, hatchlings (newly hatched babies), half-grown juveniles and adults. Some of the eggs even contain fossilized fragments of embryonic bones. Many *Protoceratops* eggs have been found in the Gobi Desert; they are elongated in shape, 20 centimetres or so in length, and have roughly wrinkled shells. Even more interesting, they were found in nests in the sand in clutches of up to eighteen eggs, arranged in three circles one within the other.

The stegosaurs or plated dinosaurs

Altogether different from the horned dinosaurs were the plated dinosaurs, the Stegosauria. The most familiar is *Stegosaurus* itself ('covering lizard' or 'roof lizard'; *see* Plate 2); this animal lived in Late Jurassic times (140 million years ago) in western North America. Related forms have been found elsewhere – including England – in rocks of the same age or a little older, and recent evidence suggests that the stegosaurs survived (but only just!) through most of the Cretaceous.

Stegosaurus was 6 metres or more in length and would have tipped the scales at nearly 2 tonnes. The tiny, narrow head, only 40 centimetres long, had small weak teeth and contained a brain no bigger than a walnut. The front legs were very short and the back legs very long, more than twice as long, so that the animal stood very high at the hips. The feature that makes *Stegosaurus* instantly recognizable is the double row of enormous bony plates that ran along its back and tail; they were probably arranged in a zigzag fashion and stood almost upright, although it has recently been suggested that the arrangement was actually very different and that they lay flat in (or on) the skin. No one really knows what they were for, but they may somehow have helped *Stegosaurus* defend itself against attack by flesh-eaters like *Allosaurus*. Again an alternative suggestion is that these plates – in this case supposedly erect – were abundantly supplied with blood-vessels and acted as heat exchangers, absorbing heat from the sun when the creature was too cold and radiating heat outwards when the animal became too warm. In any event, *Stegosaurus* was better able to defend itself by lashing out with its thick strong tail; the end bore two pairs of sharp spikes, each nearly 1 metre long, which together formed an extremely dangerous weapon.

Kentrosaurus, a plated dinosaur from the Upper Jurassic
of Tanzania. Typical length 5 metres.

Polacanthus, an armoured dinosaur from the Lower Cretaceous of southern England. Typical length 4 metres.

The ankylosaurs or armoured dinosaurs

Despite the apparent success of *Stegosaurus* and its relatives – they were fairly common in certain widely separated parts of the world – plated dinosaurs became extremely rare in the Cretaceous. Conversely, the third group of non-ornithopod Ornithischia – the armoured dinosaurs or Ankylosauria, of which we have only the faintest trace in the Jurassic – then became much more abundant. An early ankylosaur was *Polacanthus* ('many-spined'; *see* Plate 5), known from a single specimen found in the Lower Cretaceous (115 million years old) of the Isle of Wight. Its head is missing but the whole animal was probably a little over 4 metres long. The creature had a low flattened body and powerful limbs; a double row of large, upwardly projecting spines ran along the back, a solid bony shield covered the hips, and a double row of smaller stegosaur-like plates protected the tail. *Hylaeosaurus* ('forest lizard'), one of Owen's three original Dinosauria (*see* p.51), seems to have been an animal of the same sort; but the type specimen has never been removed from the Sussex slab in which it was found, nearly 150 years ago, and it is therefore still partly encased in rock. At last, however, the bones are scheduled for extraction from the matrix by treatment with acetic acid in order to prove or disprove a recent suggestion that *Hylaeosaurus* and *Polacanthus* are in fact two specimens of the same genus, perhaps even of the same species; they are in any case of the same age. If they do belong to the same genus, then the name *Hylaeosaurus* must be used for both of them; this is because it is the older (1832 as against 1882).

A later, even more heavily armoured dinosaur – a veritable 'reptilian tank' – was *Ankylosaurus* ('stiff lizard') from the Upper Cretaceous of western North America. About 4.5 metres long, it had a broad blunt head, an even broader massive body and short solid legs. The whole of its upper surface – head, neck, back and tail – was covered in a heavy but flexible armour, consisting mainly of thick oval plates of bone set close together in a leathery skin. The back end of the skull was drawn out into two pairs of pyramidal bony spikes, short but sharp, projecting to either side of the head. The thick and powerful tail ended in an enormous bony club. Since the animal's teeth were blunt and weak it would doubtless crouch down if attacked, its legs tucked under its body and the whole of its unprotected lower side pressed close to the ground. The tail-club would then be swung violently at its attacker with deadly effect.

Other areas where ankylosaurs have been found include Mongolia, India, Rumania and (very recently) Queensland.

Scelidosaurus

The last dinosaur to be described, *Scelidosaurus* ('limb lizard'; *see* Plate 3), does not fit neatly into any of our groups. It has often been regarded as an ancestral stegosaur; it might be an ancestral ankylosaur; it could well be neither! Found in the Lower Jurassic of Dorset (about 185 million

Scolosaurus, an armoured dinosaur from the Upper
Cretaceous of Alberta. Typical length 6 metres.

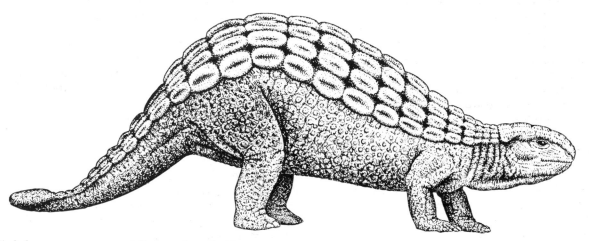

Ankylosaurus, an armoured dinosaur from the Upper
Cretaceous of western North America. Typical length 4.5
metres.

Scelidosaurus, a quadrupedal ornithischian from the
Lower Jurassic of Dorset. Typical length 4 metres.

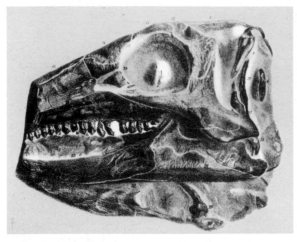

The skull of *Scelidosaurus*, lacking only the snout:
Above. After the initial preparation in about 1860. (This
illustration is a contemporary drawing.) The skull is still
largely encased in rock.
Below. After complete preparation in acetic acid during
the nineteen-sixties. Every minute detail of the skull is
now visible, even such structures as the replacement
teeth on the inner sides of the functional dentition. The
length of the skull, as preserved, is 17.5 centimetres, the
length of the lower jaw is 18.3 centimetres; the end of the
snout is missing.

years old), it was the earliest ornithischian
dinosaur known until the discovery of *Heterodontosaurus* in 1962. The first *Scelidosaurus* to
be discovered was described by Richard Owen
in 1861; the only other known, very much
smaller, was found in 1955. The larger individual was a heavily built quadruped some 4
metres long with a small head and weak jaws.
Its most noteworthy feature is the armour of
solid bony plates embedded in the skin, especially along the middle of the neck, back and
tail; some of the plates are of a very complicated
shape. At present this specimen too is being
taken out of the rock completely by chemical
means and we hope that we shall soon know
much more about its anatomy (and hence its
relationships) than we do now. Indeed, it is true
to say that we learn as much from our old
specimens, studied by modern methods, as we do
from the new ones just collected.

16 · Warm blood and the dinosaurs

In Chapter 9 we mentioned the unfortunate fact that, when a fossil animal is assigned to a particular class, people tend to assume automatically *and without justification* that it possessed all the class characters possessed by the modern members of that class. Thus, having decided that certain fossils should be called mammals because of the characters of their skeletons (especially their lower jaws), such people take it for granted that those animals, when alive, had all the other characters of a *modern* mammal – including warm blood. All fossil birds too are likewise assumed to have been warm-blooded. In the same way it has been assumed that anything classified as a reptile possessed all the other characters of a modern reptile – including cold blood; this applied to *all* fossil reptiles, whether or not they were on their way towards becoming mammals or birds.

There is no doubt whatever that the dinosaurs, judged by their skeletons, were reptiles. Therefore it was believed (quite without reason, although not necessarily wrongly) that dinosaurs must have been cold-blooded like all the reptiles of today. Everyone took this for granted; no one questioned it at all. Then, about thirty years ago, a different point of view began to appear, suggesting that dinosaurs might have been *warm*-blooded. At first nobody took much notice of this, but more recently still, within the last ten years or so, scientists have published more and more articles on this problem. Some state quite definitely that dinosaurs *were* warm-blooded, others state the opposite just as firmly, and the matter is now being hotly debated at scientific meetings and in scientific journals. The wiser palaeontologists, however, just sit on the fence and say that this question cannot be answered at present, for some of the evidence points in one direction and some of it in the other.

Let us ask ourselves – what is the advantage of being warm-blooded? It is simply that no four-legged backboned animal can produce much energy and be really active unless it is warm. When we talk about a mammal as being 'warm-blooded' we really mean that it is warm-blooded *all the time*; it makes its own heat by burning up food in its muscles, and it prevents that heat from escaping by means of an outside insulation of fur and perhaps fat under the skin. On the other hand, when we call a reptile 'cold-blooded' we mean that it relies upon the outside world to heat up its body – for example, after a cold night a lizard has to bask in the morning sun until it is warmed right through. The warm-blooded animal can therefore remain active throughout the night, in cold weather, even during a long cold winter, and it can live in countries that are too cold for 'cold-blooded' animals. It can also produce energy more quickly than a 'cold-blooded' animal, even if the latter is thoroughly warm, and it can go on producing it for longer; it can therefore be more active over a longer period, even in cold conditions, and it can obtain and eat more food. (Against this, the warm-blooded animal *needs* much more food in order to do all this and, in cold weather, to produce the necessary heat.) Some cold-blooded amphibians and reptiles avoid the difficulties of a long cold winter by going into hibernation – during which time they use very little energy at all. Some warm-blooded mammals also hibernate if the supply of food is insufficient to keep up their body temperature, becoming in effect cold-blooded for the duration of the winter.

Now let us take a look at some of the reasons that have been put forward for believing that dinosaurs were warm-blooded. The first argument ever thought of went something like this. The earliest dinosaurs and the earliest mammals both appeared at about the same time (Late Triassic – *see* Chapter 4); and it was the dinosaurs that became the big and important land animals for the next 140 million years, not the mammals. But the mammals – by definition – were warm-blooded. It is a great advantage to have warm blood; surely the dinosaurs could not have gained supremacy over the mammals unless they had been warm-blooded too?

One of the most striking things about a

dinosaur is the way it stood or ran, with its legs in a vertical plane beneath its body – the 'fully improved' stance and gait referred to in Chapter 1, which is, in fact, the absolute diagnostic of the dinosaurs. This is not at all like the sprawling posture of most modern reptiles, with the belly on the ground and the legs projecting sideways – particularly noticeable when the reptile is at rest. Indeed, the posture of the dinosaur must have been very like that of a modern running mammal such as a dog. The only animals alive today with the 'fully erect' posture of the legs – birds and mammals – are *all* warm-blooded, which suggests – so it is argued – that the dinosaurs must have been warm-blooded too.

Again, dinosaurs have long legs. There is not much point in having long legs unless they can be used for fast running. To maintain a high speed over a long distance, however, the animal must produce a great deal of energy, and it must keep on producing it for a long time. It is said that only warm-blooded animals can do that; cold-blooded animals can produce energy quite quickly and they can run quite fast, but only in short bursts.

There are other ways in which dinosaurs resemble modern running mammals rather than modern reptiles. For example, there may be some similarity in the microscopic structure of their bones. Dinosaur bone, like mammal bone, also has more blood-vessels running through it than have the bones of, say, a lizard or a crocodile.

A new argument put forward recently states that a warm-blooded carnivore needs far more meat than a cold-blooded carnivore, most of it as 'fuel' for maintaining its higher temperature and more active life. This means that a given quantity of meat (i.e., a given number of prey animals killed by the carnivores) will not supply nearly as many warm-blooded carnivores as it would cold-blooded ones. We may therefore count all the large fossil animals found in a particular stratum, carnivores and prey animals separately, and calculate the former as a percentage of the whole; a small percentage of carnivores will mean that they must have been greedy eaters and therefore warm-blooded, a large percentage will mean that they must have had modest appetites and presumably cold

blood. In theory this is an interesting idea, but in practice it simply cannot work; the proportion of carnivores to prey in a fossil sample is affected by so many other factors that it cannot possibly give a true indication of the proportion of carnivores among the living animals of the time. For example, some types of animal may have become fossilized much more readily than others: perhaps they usually died in the swamps rather than in the uplands, perhaps their flesh had an unpleasant taste so that other animals would tend to leave their carcasses alone, or perhaps their bones were much stouter and more resistant to damage and decay. Again, the person who collected the fossils might have been a specialist in one particular sort, so he might not have bothered to pick up all the specimens that did not interest *him*. Finally, let us suppose that the living population of the predators remained fixed at a certain number; then it is obvious that the longer each animal lived, the fewer would have died each year and the smaller would have been the number of skeletons available for fossilization.

In any case, there are many palaeontologists who do not accept the sort of evidence we have just been looking at. Not only do they try to pick holes in it but they also put forward their own evidence – evidence which points in the opposite direction. Thus it is argued that an enormous bulky animal like a dinosaur can keep the temperature of its body fairly constant without having to produce its own body heat and without any outside insulation at all, simply because it is so big. The temperature of the body will indeed go up and down as the surrounding air becomes warmer or cooler, but it will do so very, very slowly; and, if the animal is living in a warm climate that changes very little, then the variations in the animal's body temperature will be so small as hardly to matter. All this, however, would not be true of the many small dinosaurs.

Greatly enlarged sections through bone:
Above lizard;
Middle dinosaur;
Below mammal.
The lizard bone is more highly magnified than the other two; the 'holes' in the top section contained the bone cells and correspond to the *small* black holes in the others. It can nevertheless be seen that the dinosaur, like the mammal but unlike the lizard, possesses concentric *Haversian systems.*

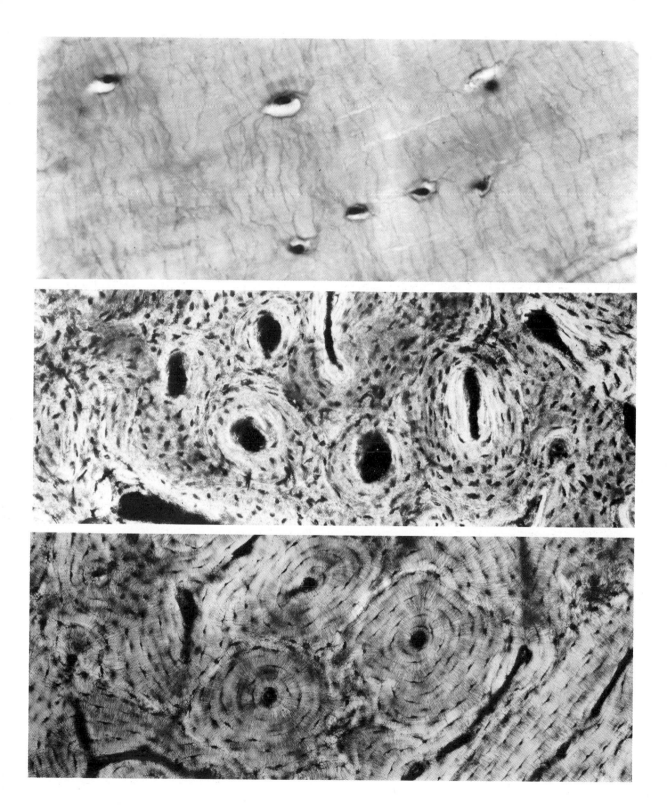

Another scientist believes (for exactly the same reason) that newly hatched dinosaurs could not have kept their body temperature constant, for they were small and naked and, as far as we know, were not kept warm by their parents. If they could not have maintained a constant temperature they could not have been warm-blooded.

It has also been said that the small size of the brain in dinosaurs suggests a rather sluggish way of life and therefore cold blood.

In conclusion, it is interesting to note that the same evidence has been used by both sides to 'prove' their opposite points of view. Sauropod dinosaurs had enormous bodies, small heads and weak teeth. It has been stated that such animals could not have eaten enough food to obtain sufficient energy to keep their body temperature high. But it has also been said that only warm-blooded animals would have had the energy to stand for hours gathering the vast quantities of food they needed!

17 · Dinosaurs and birds

Archaeopteryx gliding

Compsognathus, a coelurosaur from the Upper Jurassic of southern Germany. Length about 65 centimetres.

A dinosaur – as most people think of it – would seem to bear little likeness to a bird. True, an ostrich dinosaur does bear a certain similarity to an ostrich; a duck-billed dinosaur swimming in the lake might look from a distance as though it were a gigantic duck; and, less convincingly, a parrot dinosaur does have a parrot-like beak. Moreover, as far as we know, both birds and dinosaurs lay (or laid) eggs, arranging them in clutches. Can these similarities mean that there is any relationship between the two groups?

The answer to that question is certainly 'no'; the similarities mentioned are purely coincidental. It nevertheless appears that there may be a close relationship between dinosaurs and birds, closer than anyone realized until a few years ago. Indeed, there is now a respectable theory that birds are the direct descendants of coelurosaurian dinosaurs, the small, lightly built, fast-running bipeds that we discussed in Chapter 12. It has even been said that birds *are* dinosaurs, still living today.

Before we can discuss this interesting idea any further we must introduce *Archaeopteryx*. *Archaeopteryx* ('ancient wing') is the oldest fossil bird known; it lived as long ago as the Late Jurassic, some 150 to 145 million years before the present. The first two specimens were found in southern Germany in 1861 and 1877, and for nearly a century no more were discovered. Recently, however, three more have turned up, so now there are five altogether.

What is particularly interesting about *Archaeopteryx* is that it looks like a reptile which is actually in the process of evolving into a bird, or, to put it the other way round, like a bird which has not yet completed its change from reptilian ancestors. More simply, it shows a mixture of reptilian and bird-like characters. The very first *Archaeopteryx*, the 1861 specimen, is probably the most valuable fossil in the world; it belongs to the Natural History Museum in London, where it is kept in conditions of the strictest security. (The specimen on exhibition is a beautifully made cast in glass-fibre.)

The London *Archaeopteryx* (main slab). It measures 35
centimetres, as preserved, from the tips of the left
metacarpals to the end of the bony tail.

a	ankle	sk	bones of the skull roof (inner side)
f	feathers (on fore-limbs and tail)	t	tail
fa	bones of the fore-arm (radius and ulna)	th	thigh-bone (femur)
ft	hind foot	ti	bone of the lower leg (tibia)
h	bones of the 'hand' (metacarpals)	ua	bone of the upper arm (humerus)
p	pubis	v	vertebrae (backbone)
sb	shoulder-blade	w	wishbone

The Berlin *Archaeopteryx* (main slab). This specimen is so complete and well preserved that the photograph requires neither annotation nor explanation. Although its position is different from that of the London specimen, the corresponding measurement is almost the same (34 centimetres).

Part of the feathered tail of the London *Archaeopteryx*, with a row of quills along each side of the vertebral column

The left hind-foot of the London *Archaeopteryx*, with the opposable first toe

The most noticeable bird-like features of *Archaeopteryx* are its feathers and its wishbone – two characters which are absolutely typical of birds and have never been found in anything else. The feathers are preserved only as impressions on the very fine-grained limestone in which the fossils were buried; yet, in their arrangement and their structure, even under the microscope, they are exactly like the feathers of a modern bird. It is because of its feathers that *Archaeopteryx* is classified as a bird. The wishbone or merrythought of a bird is a single bone familiar to everyone who eats chicken; it is supposed to have been formed by the growing together of the two collar-bones, left and right, which in other animals remain separate. In *Archaeopteryx* the wishbone is not much like a chicken's, it is more like a boomerang in shape. It has also been said that *Archaeopteryx* has wings, a perching foot, and a pubis pointing downwards and *backwards* (like that of the 'bird-hipped' dinosaurs, as explained in Chapter 10, but the resemblance is purely superficial).

On the other hand, *Archaeopteryx* has kept a large number of reptile characters which the birds of today no longer possess. Most noticeable of all is its long bony tail, with large feathers arranged down each side. (Some modern birds seem to have long tails, but such tails consist only of feathers; pluck the feathers and nothing remains but the 'parson's nose'.) Another important difference is that *Archaeopteryx* still has teeth; no living bird has teeth, just a horny bill. The fore-limb or wing still has three clawed fingers at its end, which nearly all modern birds have lost almost entirely. And there are other differences, too numerous to mention.

At the same time there is an equally large number of bird characters that *Archaeopteryx* has *not* got. One of these is a strong keel to the breast-bone for the attachment of powerful flying muscles (the white meat of the chicken breast is the flying muscles, the bony plate between those muscles is the keel); but not all birds have this. Other special 'birdy' characters lacking in *Archaeopteryx* are the air-spaces within the bones (which help to lighten the whole animal) and an enlarged brain.

There is therefore little doubt that *Archaeo-*

The wishbone of the London *Archaeopteryx*. All the other structures are ribs and vertebrae, except for the left scapula (shoulder-blade) running in a diagonal curve across the bottom left-hand corner.

The front of the upper jaw of the London *Archaeopteryx*, showing five teeth. (This bone is on the counterslab, not the main slab.) Combined span of the five teeth 12.5 millimetres.

pteryx is a bird; but it is a very primitive bird, still possessing many reptile characters and not yet showing many new characters found in all modern birds. The important question is: from which particular reptiles did it come?

The suggestion that it evolved from coelurosaurian dinosaurs is not new. It was first put forward many years ago, but at that time most people agreed that it could not be correct because of one simple objection. *Archaeopteryx* had a wishbone – the two collar-bones joined together – but all dinosaurs were thought to have lost their collar-bones. A dinosaur without collar-bones could hardly have given rise to an *Archaeopteryx* which still possessed those elements, albeit somewhat modified to form a wishbone!

Recently, however, this old idea has been revived and brought up to date. It is now known that a few dinosaurs – coelurosaurian dinosaurs – do have collar-bones; and, even where no collar-bones have been found with the fossil, this need not mean that the living animal did

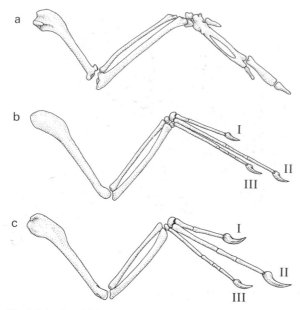

not possess any. Perhaps it did, and up till now no one has discovered them; or perhaps its collar-bones were made only of soft connective tissue, not proper bone, and were therefore never fossilized. Thus it would seem that the chief objection to the dinosaur theory – the *only* objection – is not really an objection at all.

It has also been claimed that the fore-limb skeleton of *Archaeopteryx* is not in the least like that of a modern bird's wing but is uncannily like the fore-limb of a coelurosaur in almost every detail. (Nevertheless there is no doubt that *Archaeopteryx* was capable of flapping flight; its flight feathers were asymmetrical, like those of modern flying birds, and unlike the symmetrical quills of non-flyers.) The foot,

The fore-limb skeletons of:
(a)   A modern bird (raven);
(b)   *Archaeopteryx*;
(c)   The dinosaur *Deinonychus*.

The Eichstätt *Archaeopteryx* (main slab); found in 1951. It measures 21.5 centimetres, as preserved, from the tips of the right metacarpals to the end of the bony tail.

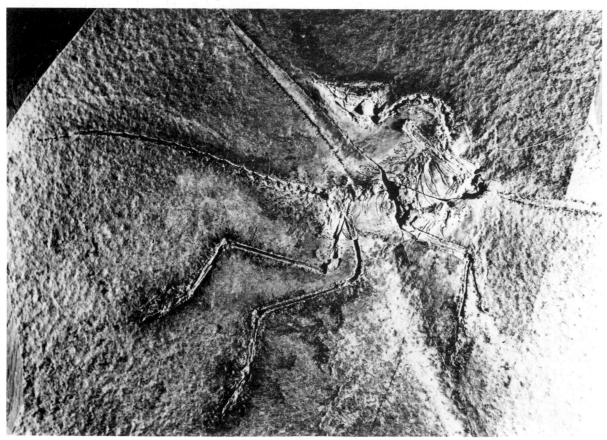

Restoration of *Archaeopteryx* as a ground-dweller

Restoration of *Archaeopteryx* as a tree-dweller

it is said, was not a perching foot but has almost exactly the same structure as the running foot of the coelurosaurs; and the pubis seems to be directed, not downwards and backwards, but almost straight downwards. The only important bird-like characters which *Archaeopteryx* has been left with are the feathers and the wishbone!

Altogether, so it is asserted, the skeleton of *Archaeopteryx* resembles a coelurosaur skeleton in twenty-one specialized characters. It has even been said that *Archaeopteryx* is just 'a coelurosaur with feathers'; that seems to be almost true, for one of the newer *Archaeopteryx* specimens (found in 1951) was thought to be a small coelurosaur skeleton until someone noticed its feather impressions more than twenty years later. Some specialists consider that the similarities between *Archaeopteryx* and coelurosaurs are so many and so detailed that they cannot *all* be coincidental and they therefore believe that *Archaeopteryx* and all later birds *did* evolve from coelurosaurian dinosaurs.

This belief, nevertheless, is not without its problems, and there is a considerable minority of reputable workers who find it unacceptable. One alternative view (the conventional one, held almost universally until a few years ago) is that birds evolved directly from thecodontians; another is that the origin of birds is more closely connected with the earliest crocodilians than with dinosaurs. Paradoxically enough, the suggestion that the birds' closest relatives might be the 'bird-hipped' dinosaurs is no longer supported by anyone.

Another equally important question is: how did the birds begin to fly? Here we have two completely different ideas. One is that the ancestors of the birds were able to climb trees, perhaps even lived up in the branches. Soon they learnt to jump from bough to bough; then they began to use their outstretched fore-limbs (which were perhaps already feathered) as parachutes to break their fall; next they started to glide; and finally they found out how to move their fore-limbs up and down in proper flapping flight. The opposite idea is that the ancestors of the birds were running bipeds (this fits in better with the belief that birds evolved from coelurosaurian dinosaurs) and that, for some reason or other, they stretched out their fore-limbs as they ran, eventually getting enough 'lift' to take off from the ground. It has recently been suggested that the ancestors of *Archaeopteryx* began to use their feathered fore-limbs in this manner in order to trap the insects upon which they fed. There are many arguments for and many arguments against both the 'tree-jumping' theory and the 'ground-running' theory; scientists are still arguing hotly about them and, to be honest, no one as yet has provided any absolutely convincing evidence one way or the other.

Yet another idea is that the first flying birds flew only reluctantly and very badly; they would run bipedally along branches to escape pursuing predators, launch themselves clumsily into the air and flutter erratically down into the undergrowth. The advantage of this type of behaviour was that its very unpredictability would perplex the hunter and improve the bird's chances of avoiding capture. After such unimpressive beginnings, so the theory continues, natural selection would favour those individuals that could fly farther, landing not too close to the predator, and, in this manner, the evolutionary process would gradually improve the powers of flight.

The newly formulated theory that birds evolved from coelurosaurian dinosaurs has led some of its supporters to propose certain changes in the classification of all these animals. Each of them has put forward his own scheme, but the general idea has been to place the birds and the dinosaurs (in some cases all the dinosaurs, in others just the theropods) into the same group. This combined group of closely related animals would then be called either 'Dinosaurs' or

The Greater Coucal (*Centropus sinensis*) of China and the northern parts of the Indian sub-continent. This bird is a poor flyer whose erratic and unpredictable behaviour is not unlike that postulated for *Archaeopteryx* by some scientists.

'Birds' according to taste. It should be noted, however, that such reclassifications require the acceptance of two or three fairly novel ideas: dinosaurs gave rise to birds, dinosaurs (like birds) were warm-blooded, and (where *all* the dinosaurs are involved) dinosaurs form but a single group instead of two. Since none of these ideas has as yet gained general acceptance – and, indeed, they may never do so – it follows that the suggested reclassifications are hopelessly premature and cannot be taken seriously. They will, in any case, be ignored by most people; after all, does it really make sense to call *Tyrannosaurus rex* a bird, or a sparrow a dinosaur? If the latter idea caught on we might well have to change some of our proverbs: 'Dinosaurs of a feather flock together', and 'A dinosaur in the hand is worth two in the bush'. The dawn chorus of the dinosaurs would waken us early in the morning, we should visit the Dinosaur House at the zoo to see the humming-dinosaurs flitting lightly from flower to flower, and we should round off our excursion by lunching on Dinosaur Marengo in the Members' Restaurant. But, in truth, we need not fear that such absurdities will prevail. Common sense and popular usage are far more powerful influences on language than is scientific pedantry – especially when the latter is based on such insubstantial grounds.

18 · Geographical distribution

We have already explained, in Chapter 7, that the remains of dinosaurs are found only in sedimentary rocks of Late Triassic to Late Cretaceous age – that is, between about 205 million and 65 million years old; and we have also explained that they generally occur in freshwater or dry-land deposits, only rarely in sediments formed in the sea. Dinosaurs seem to have been widely distributed in the Mesozoic world, for they have been found in all the present continents (except Antarctica, where, as already noted, they probably lie beneath the ice with little hope of discovery in the near future). It therefore follows that the pattern of their present-day distribution is indicated more or less accurately by a geological map showing where Mesozoic rocks of suitable type are exposed at the surface. The most important dinosaur areas in the world today were mentioned in Chapter 6.

This does not mean, however, that there were no dinosaurs living in other parts of the Mesozoic world. Dinosaur-bearing deposits may be present elsewhere, lying beneath accumulations of younger rocks; thus, for example, the main exposure of Jurassic rocks in England (many of them containing dinosaurs) runs in a broad band from Dorset to Yorkshire, but to the east of that band great thicknesses of Jurassic rocks underlie the later deposits. Alternatively it may be that dinosaur-bearing strata were once present *above* the older rocks now exposed at the surface but were long ago removed by uplift and erosion. Taking all these factors into account and bearing in mind that dinosaurs were land animals, almost certainly unable to cross wide stretches of sea, it is obvious that their distribution – not just the distribution of dinosaurs considered as a whole, but the different distributions of the particular sorts of dinosaur – may give us some hint of the way the continents were arranged when those dinosaurs were still living; it may also give some indication of the climates of those continents at that time. (The distribution of dinosaurs, of course, must be studied in conjunction with the distribution of other contemporary fossils, vertebrate and invertebrate, plants as well as animals, marine as well as freshwater and terrestrial.) And, conversely, our knowledge of the geography of any particular time – the *palaeogeography* – should help us to understand the pattern of dinosaur distribution.

To be honest, we must admit that the distribution of dinosaurs and their immediate ancestors, the thecodontians, is not especially helpful in this connection (except in the Upper Cretaceous, as detailed below). Twenty-five years ago it seemed that the respective Triassic faunas of the Northern and Southern Hemispheres were quite characteristic and distinct from each other; this suggested that they lived on two great land-masses, 'Laurasia' (North America, Europe and Asia) and 'Gondwanaland' (South America, Africa, Arabia, Madagascar, India, Australia, New Zealand and Antarctica), sepa-

The exposure of the Jurassic in England (black). The stippled area indicates where Jurassic rocks underlie the later deposits.

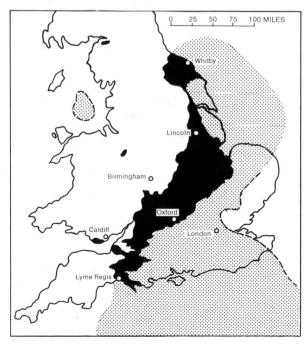

A world map of the more important places where the remains of dinosaurs have been found. There is no indication of relative abundance; some of the symbols represent whole areas rich in dinosaurs from which large faunas have been taken, others represent the discovery of a single bone fragment.

Legend:

● U. Cretaceous
○ L. Cretaceous
■ U. Jurassic
∗ L. Jurassic
▲ M. & U. Triassic

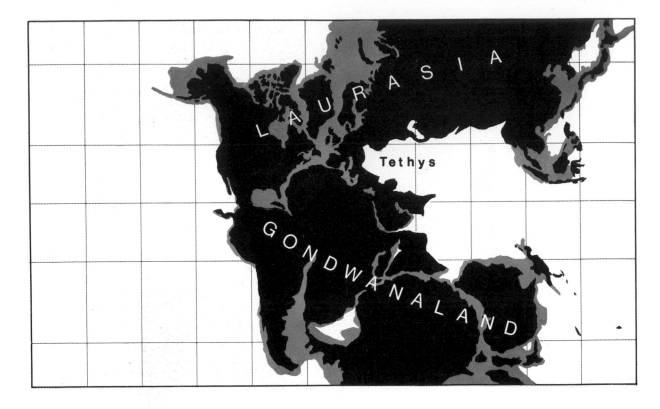

rated from each other by an impassable geo-graphical barrier which was probably a sea running east and west (called the Tethys). For example, very similar Middle Triassic theco-dontians from Brazil and Tanzania belonged to a family (Prestosuchidae) unknown in the Nor-thern Hemisphere, while, conversely, members of another family (Stagonolepididae) had been found fairly frequently in the Upper Trias of the U.S.A. (south-west and east), in Scotland and in Germany but not south of the Equator. This state of affairs, however, did not last. The negative evidence, the absence of prestosuchids from the Northern Hemisphere and of stagono-lepidids from the Southern, was later disproved by unmistakable discoveries in Switzerland and Argentina respectively.

Further discoveries have made it increas-ingly obvious that there is no essential differ-ence between the Triassic faunas of Laurasia and of Gondwanaland. We may therefore pre-sume that the dinosaur ancestors of Triassic times and, in the Late Triassic, the dinosaurs themselves were able to walk without hin-

A map of the world as it was 200 million years ago, in Late Triassic times. The grey areas around the margins of the black continents are the continental shelves, beneath the sea at present but not necessarily submerged at other times.

drance from one supercontinent to the other. This implies that the two supercontinents were somehow connected, that neither the Tethys nor any other geographical barrier – such as an impenetrable mountain range – separated them completely. (The figure above is a map of the world in Triassic times, reconstructed by palaeogeographers according to the best evid-ence available; it shows the connection between Laurasia and Gondwanaland as lying in what is now the region of the North and Central Atlan-tic, between North America and Spain on one side and South America and Africa on the other.) The cosmopolitan nature of the dinosaur fauna also shows that there were no climatic barriers (belts of extreme heat or cold, rainfall or drought, with consequent lack of suitable

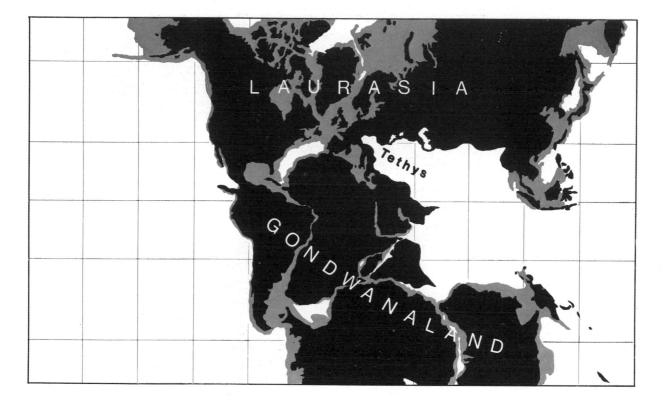

A map of the world as it was 160 million years ago, in mid-Jurassic times

vegetable food) which might likewise have caused total separation of the dinosaurs into two differing assemblages.

Until very recently, then, it was generally accepted without question that the dinosaur faunas of the Jurassic and Cretaceous were, like those of the Trias, more or less uniform in all parts of the globe; traces of dinosaurs have been found in nearly every part, including places like Alaska and Spitzbergen. It has even been claimed that remains found in regions now widely separated (such as Colorado and Tanzania, Argentina and Madagascar, Alberta and Mongolia) belonged to the same genera. This suggested not only that all the major land-masses were somehow interconnected throughout the Mesozoic but also – since nearly every-

one then accepted unquestioningly that dinosaurs were cold-blooded – that the climate was everywhere warm, even in places that now lie within the Arctic Circle, until the Cretaceous was drawing to its close. It also seemed probable that there was little difference in temperature between summer and winter.

As far as the Jurassic was concerned this may well have been true. It has to be admitted that an incipient Central Atlantic was then beginning to separate Laurasia from Gondwanaland and that the two supercontinents were themselves beginning to split up; it nevertheless seems that land animals could still migrate between North America and Africa via Europe, for the Late Jurassic dinosaurs in the Morrison Formation of Colorado, South Dakota and neighbouring states are remarkably similar to those from Tendaguru in Tanzania (both faunas allegedly including, for example, the gigantic sauropods *Barosaurus* and *Brachiosaurus* and the small ornithopod *Dryosaurus*). It also seems probable that there was a good overland route between Siberia and Alaska.

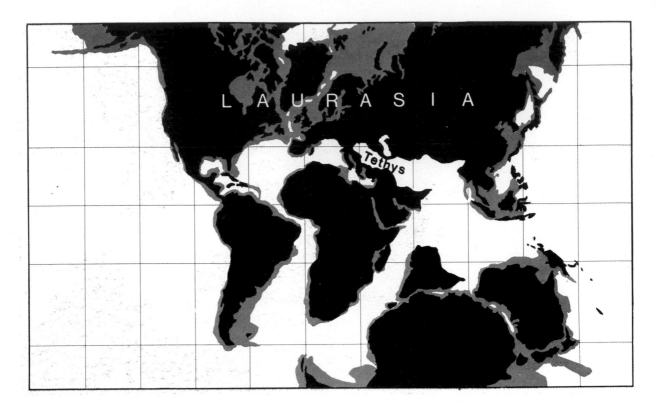

A map of the world as it was 100 million years ago, in mid-Cretaceous times

In the Cretaceous, however, recent studies have shown that the picture is not so simple and that the dinosaurs really do help our palaeogeographical speculations. It is of little use to pay much attention to groups of dinosaurs that were already established world-wide in Jurassic times; these would obviously be capable of continued existence in all parts of the world during the Cretaceous, whether or not the connections between those parts were maintained. On the other hand, there are several *new* dinosaur groups in the Cretaceous, some of which do not appear until well into that period; and, if any of those appeared first on land-masses which had already become isolated, it might be presumed that they would not have been able to spread to other land-masses. The families concerned are (Saurischia) the dromaeosaurids, ornithomimids and tyrannosaurids and (Ornithischia) the hadrosaurids, psittacosaurids and pachycephalosaurids, together with all the several families of the horned and armoured dinosaurs. All these families are well known in Laurasia, often from scores of well-preserved specimens; but records of their presence in Gondwanaland, by contrast, are all (save one) based on a few inadequate scraps which do not allow a satisfactory determination and may therefore be discounted. The one exception is the skeleton of a primitive duckbill in the Upper Cretaceous of Argentina. Such a distribution suggests that there was no longer any good connection between the two supercontinents in Cretaceous times, although somewhere there must have been a migration route which allowed the duckbill to struggle through. (That passage might even have involved a short swim, for hadrosaurs were better adapted to a semi-aquatic existence than were other dinosaurs.) Further, the route might also have been closed well before the end of the Cretaceous, for there

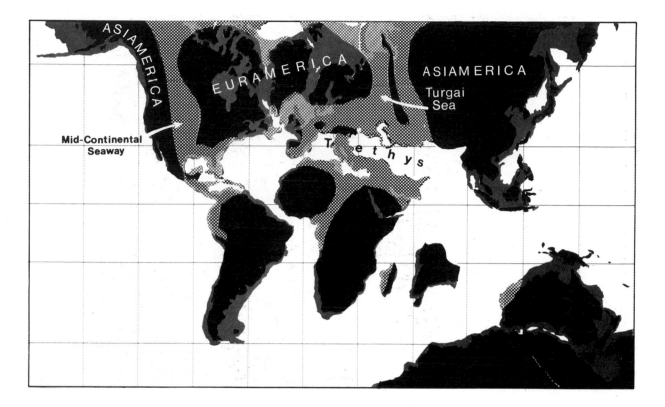

A map of the world as it was 80 million years ago, in Late Cretaceous times. Epicontinental seas are shown by white stipple on the black continents; they divide the former Laurasia into Asiamerica and Euramerica.

is as yet no evidence that the more advanced hadrosaurs, which evolved later than the primitive forms, ever succeeded in entering Gondwanaland.

A slightly more detailed study of the Upper Cretaceous dinosaurs of Laurasia demonstrates the remarkable fact that the fauna of eastern North America is like that of Europe, while the fauna of western North America is like that of Asia. This confirms a deduction made from other evidence, that in Late Cretaceous times North America and Eurasia were each split into two by a shallow *epicontinental* sea running from north to south. These two seas, the Mid-Continental Seaway and the Turgai Sea respectively, created two new continents in the Northern Hemisphere, 'Asiamerica' (Asia plus western North America) and 'Euramerica' (eastern North America plus Europe). Their existence accords with the fact that reliable records of dromaeosaurids, tyrannosaurids, pachycephalosaurids, protoceratopids, ceratopids and pachyrhinosaurids are from Asiamerica only. Of the four subfamilies of the hadrosaurs, only the most primitive, the Hadrosaurinae, has been found in both land-masses; it first appeared in the Early Cretaceous (presumably before both seaways had formed) and was thus able to extend its range throughout Laurasia, but the other three subfamilies evolved from it in Asiamerica in the Late Cretaceous (presumably *after* the formation of the seaways) and were therefore confined to that continent. Likewise the more primitive of the two ankylosaur families (the Nodosauridae) lived – like the Hadrosaurinae – in both Euramerica and Asiamerica in Early Cretaceous times; but the more advanced family (the Ankylosauridae) appears to have lived only in the Late Cretaceous in Asiamerica, where it eventually superseded its older relatives. Thus, by latest Late Cretaceous times, the Ankylosauridae were the only ankylosaurs surviving in Asiamerica, the Nodosauridae being confined to Euramerica.

No one has yet explained the interesting fact that the Late Cretaceous dinosaurs of Asiamerica were so abundant and diverse, evolving rapidly to produce a number of entirely new families, while their contemporaries in Euramerica were so few and conservative.

Towards the very end of Late Cretaceous time the advanced ceratopians like *Triceratops*, one of the last of the dinosaurs, became exceedingly numerous in western North America; they are almost entirely absent, however, from Asia, the only exception being a single skull bone from Mongolia. This restricted distribution could indicate a lack of exposures of uppermost Cretaceous beds in Asia, or alternatively the presence of a newly formed barrier between Siberia and Alaska – perhaps another epicontinental sea – hindering the westward migration of the ceratopids. Evidence from mammal distribution favours the latter explanation.

As for the Late Cretaceous dinosaur faunas from the various parts of Gondwanaland, it has been said that they are all very similar. Most of the dinosaurs concerned, however, belong to groups which first appeared in the Lower Cretaceous or even in the Jurassic and were already widely distributed before Gondwanaland broke up; this means that the Late Cretaceous similarities merely indicate descent from a common ancestor and do not necessarily imply the existence of contemporary land connections between the various parts of the supercontinent. In any case, the similarities are not as great as is generally believed; there are

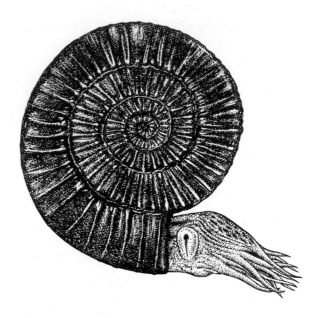

Above. Restoration of an ammonite (*see* p. 149 opposite) inside its shell. Ammonites doubtless formed an important part of the diet of large sea-reptiles like mosasaurs; indeed, their shells have been found bearing the marks of mosasaur teeth.

differences too, in particular between the South American and African faunas.

At the end of the Cretaceous all the dinosaurs died out. The next chapter, the last in the book, deals with the fascinating topic of their extinction.

Restoration of a mosasaur, one of a group of gigantic marine lizards from the Upper Cretaceous of Kansas and elsewhere. Length up to 9 metres.

19 · Death of the dinosaurs

Any expert on fossils – especially on dinosaurs – will declare that there is one question that he is asked more often than any other: 'Why did the dinosaurs die out?' The extinction of these great reptiles, some 65 million years ago, seems to hold more interest and fascination than any other problem of the prehistoric world. It is a pity that relatively few people take any interest in the *origin* of the dinosaurs, in what they evolved from and why; not only is that subject rather more important but it is also a matter on which, as we have seen, there is much better evidence.

Most people, of course, divide all animals and plants into two groups: living and extinct. They suppose that some have been successful and have therefore survived to the present day; while the others, so they believe, were unsuccessful and therefore died out. It is this second group which includes the dinosaurs. But we saw in Chapter 2 how everything is always changing, so that none of the animals and plants of long ago exists now in the same form as it possessed at the time; in that sense *all* prehistoric animals and plants are extinct. Yet they cannot all have been unsuccessful. Dinosaurs, for example, are certainly extinct, but they were not failures in the struggle for existence; the picture we painted of them in Chapter 1, of dinosaurs as generally imagined – slow, clumsy, stupid and unable to find the vast amounts of food that their enormous bodies needed – is very far from the truth. In the same way we can be sure that all the animals and plants of today will become extinct in their turn; after all, looking back at today from the future, it will be just another moment in the past – no different from any of the others.

On the other hand, we could restrict the use of the word 'extinct' to only those prehistoric species of animals and plants that died out without leaving any descendants. In that sense dinosaurs as a whole may *not* be extinct, for, as we have just seen in Chapter 17, some scientists believe that the dinosaurs were the ancestors of the birds. Nevertheless, if it is true that the birds came from the dinosaurs, it was only one particular group of the dinosaurs that they evolved from – the coelurosaurs – and rather early coelurosaurs at that. All other groups of dinosaurs, and later coelurosaurs too, really did die out without evolving into anything else; they really *are* extinct.

We have already seen that the strata of the Upper Cretaceous contain many different sorts of dinosaur, some of them – especially the plant-eaters like the duckbills and the horned ceratopians – in very large numbers. But as we continue upwards through the rocks they all disappear; eventually not a bone remains, not the smallest trace of the dinosaurs' existence. What makes it even more remarkable is that it was not only the dinosaurs of the Late Cretaceous that all died out together but also, at the same time, many other animals among them the flying pterodactyls and the great sea-reptiles known as ichthyosaurs, plesiosaurs and mosasaurs. The ammonites too disappeared at the end of Cretaceous time; these were an important group of sea-animals rather like octopuses or cuttle-fish but with coiled, often beautifully decorated shells which are found in vast numbers in many of the strata formed in the seas during the Age of Dinosaurs. None of these animals left any descendants, so that all are truly extinct. Individual species of dinosaur, of course, were dying out all the time; sometimes quite large groups vanished long before the end of dinosaur history (like the prosauropods, once so abundant, which disappeared mysteriously fairly early in the Jurassic). And right up to the end new dinosaurs were evolving to replace the earlier forms, in fact there was quite a burst of altogether new dinosaurs in the second half of the Cretaceous period. But even if the extinctions at the end of that period were not as immediate and as sudden as some people like to believe, they were none the less complete. The only reptiles to survive the end of the Cretaceous were those few groups that are still living today – the turtles and tortoises, the lizards and snakes, the crocodiles and the tuatara (*see* pp. 37–8).

Now comes the important question. What *caused* all these extinctions at one particular point in time, approximately 65 million years ago? Dozens of reasons have been suggested, some serious and sensible, others quite crazy, and yet others merely as a joke. Every year people come up with new theories on this thorny problem. The trouble is that if we are to find just *one* reason to account for them all, it would have to explain the deaths, all at the same time, of animals living on land and of animals living in the sea; but, in both cases, of only *some* of those animals, for many of the land-dwellers and many of the sea-dwellers went on living quite happily into the following period. Alas, no such one explanation exists.

However, let us take a look at some of these theories. In 1963 an American professor (Glenn Jepsen of Princeton University) listed something like forty-six of them – and there have been many more since then. Perhaps there were important changes in the environment. What was happening to world geography at the end of the Cretaceous, because of the drifting of the continents? Was it a time of mountain building, when the earth's crust was undergoing violent changes? What was happening to the climate and to the seasons and to the vegetation and to the animals without backbones? All those factors might be involved – or none of them!

As we have seen, the end of the Cretaceous was indeed a time when the two land-masses of Laurasia and Gondwanaland had nearly finished splitting up into the smaller continents we know today. Laurasia was breaking up into North America, Greenland, and Europe-plus-most of Asia; Gondwanaland was splitting into South America, Africa-plus-the Middle East, Madagascar, India, Australia and Antarctica. It is generally supposed that during the Age of Dinosaurs the climate was fairly warm, with much less difference than there is now between the temperatures at the Poles and the Equator and between the winter and summer temperatures. The changes in geography would certainly have affected both the temperatures and the rainfall. It has been variously suggested that at the end of the Cretaceous the world became hotter or colder and/or wetter or drier, and it is probably true that there was a marked increase in *latitudinal* temperature differences (i.e., according to the distance from the Equator) and in *seasonal* temperature differences (i.e., according to the time of year).

The more sensible reasons suggested for the extinction of the dinosaurs include these changes in temperature (it became too hot or too cold, for at least part of the year) and in rainfall (it became too dry, causing the disappearance of the swamps and lakes in which many of the dinosaurs are supposed to have lived, or too wet, causing floods). Movements of the earth's crust, up or down, could have produced the same effects. The Walt Disney film *Fantasia* chose to show the Cretaceous dinosaurs (including a Jurassic *Stegosaurus*!) dragging themselves hopelessly to their deaths over a hot waterless desert.

It could also have been that, towards the end of the Cretaceous, the winters became so cold that the dinosaurs – if warm-blooded – could no longer keep themselves warm enough, for they had neither fur nor feathers. Equally well, if they had been cold-blooded they would have had to stay sluggish or inactive throughout the long cold winters. Either way, they were much too large to hibernate! But once again we have the same old problem: if the cold winters caused the extinction of the dinosaurs, how was it that their relatives the crocodiles were unaffected? Was their survival perhaps due to their aquatic environment, the temperature of which would remain comparatively stable?

Other changes in the environment that have been suggested at various times as possible causes of dinosaur extinction are changes in the position of the earth's axis of spin, the reversal of the earth's magnetic field (this certainly does take place every so often, magnetic North Pole becoming South Pole and vice versa), changes in gravity, changes in the pressure or composition of the air (especially too much oxygen produced by plants) and cosmic radiation.

Perhaps the dinosaurs starved to death. Maybe there were changes in the vegetation on which they fed (although, in fact, the big change – the arrival of flowering plants in large numbers – took place in the *middle* of the Cretaceous). One interesting idea put forward in 1962 supposes that the evolution of those flowering plants was followed by the first appearance of the butterflies and moths (which, in fact, are unknown until considerably later). The caterpillars of butterflies and moths feed almost entirely on plants; today their numbers are kept down by natural enemies, notably birds, but when the caterpillars first appeared on the scene the birds had not yet realized how good they were to eat. For some time, therefore, the caterpillar population increased without check. They ate so much plant food that none remained for the plant-eating dinosaurs; the plant-eating dinosaurs died of starvation, and so the meat-eating dinosaurs which preyed on them were also without food.

Another explanation is that the dinosaurs were simply starved of one particular sort of food that was absolutely necessary to them, or of an element like calcium. On the other hand, they may have eaten too much and died of over-eating! A further possibility is that there were too many meat-eating dinosaurs; they ate all the plant-eaters and then themselves died of hunger. One popular idea is that the little mammals of the Cretaceous were very fond of dinosaur eggs and ate so many of them that the dinosaurs died out.

It has sometimes been suggested that the dinosaurs were poisoned – by poisons in the water they drank or in the plants they ate. One scientist has lately shown (by experiments with tortoises) that modern reptiles have a very poor sense of taste. If this were also true of dinosaurs they might not have been able to taste the bitter and poisonous alkaloids contained in some of the flowering plants that evolved in Late Cretaceous times and would therefore have perished.

Needless to say, there are arguments for and against every one of these innumerable theories. Other causes put forward include parasites, diseases, slipped discs, shrinking brain and greater stupidity, over-specialization and inability to change, becoming too large and 'racial old age' (whatever that may be); but, for one reason or another, these too are all open to objection. The latest idea in 1982 is that the gradual warming of the earth led to premature cataract in the eyes of the dinosaurs; they eventually became blind and perished before they were old enough to reproduce.

Among the even less likely causes suggested for the death of the dinosaurs are poison gases, volcanic dust, meteorites, comets, sunspots, God's will, mass suicide (like lemmings!) and wars. A new and respectable variation on the meteorite theme is that a large asteroid, with a diameter of 6–14 km, collided with the earth; the huge dust-cloud resulting from the impact blotted out the sun for years, destroying most plant life and indirectly causing the complete extinction of the dinosaurs. Utterly ridiculous is the idea that all the dinosaurs were killed off by cavemen, for we know that the last dinosaurs died more than 60 million years before the first man of any sort put in an appearance. The last three causes that we shall mention are raids by little green hunters in flying saucers, lack of even standing room for the dinosaurs in Noah's Ark, and sheer boredom with their prehistoric world. We regard these suggestions as jokes, but perhaps the people who first made them were quite serious.

A very thoughtful essay on the subject of dinosaur extinction, published just before this amended reprint, puts forward the unorthodox belief that there is nothing especially remarkable about that extinction. The evidence, according to this view, suggests that the number of species and their geographical range diminished relatively slowly in the last few million years of the Cretaceous, so that the final disappearance of the dinosaurs differed in no particular from that of other major groups now extinct. (Only their often vast dimensions, their sometimes bizarre appearance and the dramatic light in which we picture them have led us to think of their dying out as something rather special.) There is therefore no need to invoke any unusual event to explain their demise, certainly not an extra-terrestrial event like the occurrence of a supernova.

In summary we can only confess our supreme ignorance of the real causes of dinosaur extinction and say, quite simply: 'We don't know'. To do anything else would be unscientific. Perhaps the true answer lies in a combination of several of the ideas we have just mentioned; on the other hand, it may be something completely different. Either way, it could well be that we shall never know the answer and that, whatever else we may find out about the dinosaurs, the problem of their extinction will ever remain as one of the great unsolved mysteries of science.

An outline classification of the dinosaurs (and other archosaurs)

This classification includes *all* the archosaur genera mentioned in the text of this book and in the captions to the illustrations; it does not include any others. They are grouped into orders, suborders and infra-orders. For the sake of simplicity, however, this book has generally omitted reference to the smaller group-ings; only a few families and one subfamily have been mentioned in the text (mostly in the discussion of geographical distribution) and, accordingly, it is only those family names which appear below. All family names end in '-idae'.

Class REPTILIA
  Subclass ARCHOSAURIA
    Order THECODONTIA
      Suborder PROTEROSUCHIA
        Chasmatosaurus
        Erythrosuchus
      Suborder PSEUDOSUCHIA
        Euparkeria
        Mandasuchus
        Ticinosuchus } (Prestosuchidae)
        Scleromochlus
      Suborder AËTOSAURIA
        Desmatosuchus (Stagonolepididae)
      Suborder PHYTOSAURIA
        Rutiodon
    Order CROCODILIA
      Metriorhynchus
    Order PTEROSAURIA
      Dimorphodon
      Rhamphorhynchus
      Pterodactylus
      Pteranodon

['Dinosaurs' begin here]

    Order SAURISCHIA
      Suborder THEROPODA
        Infraorder COELUROSAURIA
          Procompsognathus
          Compsognathus
          Coelophysis
          Coelurus
          Ornithomimus (Ornithomimidae)
        Infraorder DEINONYCHOSAURIA
          Deinonychus (Dromaeosauridae)
        Infraorder uncertain
          Deinocheirus
        Infraorder CARNOSAURIA
          Megalosaurus
          Allosaurus
          Dilophosaurus
          Ceratosaurus
          Altispinax
          Spinosaurus

          Tyrannosaurus
          Tarbosaurus } (Tyrannosauridae)
      Suborder SAUROPODOMORPHA
        Infraorder PROSAUROPODA
          Anchisaurus
          Massospondylus
          Riojasaurus
          Plateosaurus
        Infraorder uncertain
          Mussaurus
        Infraorder SAUROPODA
          Cetiosaurus
          Cetiosauriscus
          Diplodocus
          Apatosaurus
          (= *Brontosaurus*?)
          Hypselosaurus
          Barosaurus
          Brachiosaurus
          'Supersaurus'
    Order ORNITHISCHIA
      Suborder ORNITHOPODA
        Lesothosaurus
        Heterodontosaurus
        Dryosaurus
        Hypsilophodon
        Thescelosaurus
        Troodon
        Camptosaurus
        Tenontosaurus
        Iguanodon
        Ouranosaurus
        Trachodon
        Anatosaurus
        Edmontosaurus
        Orthomerus
        Corythosaurus
        Kritosaurus } (Hadrosauridae)
        Lambeosaurus
        Procheneosaurus
        Saurolophus
        Parasaurolophus
        Psittacosaurus (Psittacosauridae)
        Pachycephalosaurus } (Pachycephalosauridae)
        Stegoceras

Suborder CERATOPIA
  Protoceratops (Protoceratopidae)
  Monoclonius ⎤
  Chasmosaurus ⎥
  Styracosaurus ⎬ (Ceratopidae)
  Triceratops ⎥
  Pentaceratops ⎦
  Pachyrhinosaurus (Pachyrhinosauridae)
Suborder STEGOSAURIA
  Stegosaurus
  Kentrosaurus

Suborder ANKYLOSAURIA
  Hylaeosaurus ⎤
  (= *Polacanthus*?) ⎬ (Nodosauridae)
  Panoplosaurus ⎦
  Ankylosaurus ⎤
  Euoplocephalus ⎦ (Ankylosauridae)
  Scolosaurus
Suborder uncertain
  Scelidosaurus

Acknowledgements for illustrations

Acknowledgement is due to the following persons and institutions for permission to reproduce illustrations as listed:

Plate 6 and photograph on p.107: Department of Palaeobiology, Polish Academy of Sciences, Warsaw.
Plate 7: Peabody Museum of Natural History, Yale University.
Strobilite photograph on p.20: A.A. Allen.
Lower photograph on p.29, upper left photograph on p.30, photograph on p.124: American Museum of Natural History, New York.
Lower right photomicrograph on p.31: J.G. Campbell.
Photograph on p.32: C.P. Nuttall.
Cartoon on p.39: London Express News and Feature Services.
Photograph on p.54: Institut Royal des Sciences Naturelles de Belgique, Brussels.
Upper photograph on p.55: Dinosaur National Monument.
Lower photograph on p.55, photograph on p.61, lower left photograph on p.62: A.J. Charig.

Lower photograph on p.58: Institut de Paléontologie, Paris.
Upper photograph on p.62: H.W. Ball.
Photograph on p.68: A.G. Hayward.
Lower photograph on p.71: Senckenberg Museum, Frankfurt-am-Main.
Photograph on p.105: Bayerische Staatssammlung für Paläontologie und historische Geologie, Munich.
Photographs on pp.111 and 135: Museum für Naturkunde, East Berlin.
Upper photograph on p.113: J.F. Bonaparte.
Lower photograph on p.113: J.A. Jensen.
Photograph on p.138: Jura-Museum, Eichstätt.

All other photographs are copyright of the British Museum (Natural History).

Where to see dinosaurs

By far the greatest concentration of public exhibits of mounted dinosaur skeletons (original bones or casts) is in North America. A unique display is at Dinosaur National Monument in Utah, where the bones may be seen still in the cliff-face as found (pp.54–5). Among the other more comprehensive dinosaur galleries in the U.S.A. are those at the National Museum of Natural History (Smithsonian Institution) in Washington, the American Museum of Natural History in New York, the Field Museum of Natural History in Chicago, the Carnegie Museum of Natural History in Pittsburgh, the Peabody Museum of Natural History at Yale University in New Haven, the University of Utah in Salt Lake City and the Natural History Museum of Los Angeles County. Two of the best in Canada are at the National Museum in Ottawa and the Royal Ontario Museum in Toronto.

Europe is less fortunate in this respect. The famous Dinosaur Hall at the British Museum (Natural History) in London is, at the time of publication, about to be demolished; the display has been modernized and moved elsewhere in the Museum, but, until the new East Infill Block is completed, it cannot be helped that fewer specimens will be on exhibition. Other famous dinosaur displays may be seen at the Muséum National d'Histoire Naturelle in Paris, at the Institut Royal des Sciences Naturelles de Belgique in Brussels (consisting mostly of skeletons of *Iguanodon*; see p.54), at the Senckenberg Museum in Frankfurt-am-Main and at the Museum für Naturkunde in East Berlin (*see* p.111). There is also a good exhibition in Moscow; but alas, an equally good one in Warsaw was only temporary and the specimens have now been put back into store. In China too there are extensive dinosaur displays, notably in Beijing (Peking), Shanghai and Changqing.

Our list could include many other places where it is possible to see one or two dinosaur skeletons, real or cast, or restorations of dinosaurs in life; for example, there are plaster copies of an *Iguanodon* from Bernissart at both Oxford and Cambridge Universities, and likewise replicas of *Diplodocus carnegii* may be found in such cities as Vienna and La Plata (Argentina). Indeed, the only continent without any exhibited dinosaur material is Antarctica! It will therefore be obvious that not all the exhibitions can be mentioned here.

Suggestions for further reading

CHARIG, A.J. & HORSFIELD, C.M.B (1975) *Before the Ark*. London: BBC

COLBERT, E.H. (1962) *Dinosaurs: their discovery and their world*. London: Hutchinson

COLBERT, E.H. (1965) *The Age of Reptiles*. London: Weidenfeld & Nicolson

COLBERT, E.H. (1968) *Men and Dinosaurs: the search in field and laboratory*. London: Evans

COLBERT, E.H. (1969) *Evolution of the Vertebrates*, 2nd edition. New York: Wiley

COLBERT, E.H. (1974) *Wandering Lands and Animals*. London: Hutchinson

COX, C.B. (1969) *Prehistoric Animals*. London: Hamlyn. Melbourne: Sun Books

DESMOND, A.J. (1975) *The Hot-Blooded Dinosaurs*. London: Blond & Briggs. [It is recommended that this controversial book be read only in conjunction with the present author's review of it (in *Journal of Natural History*, Jan.–Feb. 1977, pp.114–16).]

HALSTEAD, L.B. (1969) *The Pattern of Vertebrate Evolution*. Edinburgh: Oliver & Boyd

HALSTEAD, L.B. (1975) *The Evolution and Ecology of the Dinosaurs*. London: Peter Lowe

HALSTEAD, L.B. & HALSTEAD, J. (1981) *Dinosaurs*. Poole (Dorset): Blandford Press

KIELAN-JAWOROWSKA, Z. (1969) *Hunting for Dinosaurs*. Cambridge (Mass.): MIT Press

KURTÉN, B. (1968) *The Age of the Dinosaurs*. London: Weidenfeld & Nicolson

LONG, R.A. & WELLES, S.P. (1975) *All New Dinosaurs (and their Friends)*. San Francisco: Bellerophon Books

MOODY, R.T.J. (1977) *A Natural History of Dinosaurs*. London: Hamlyn

ROMER, A.S. (1956) *Osteology of the Reptiles*. Chicago: University of Chicago Press

ROMER, A.S. (1959) *The Vertebrate Story*, 4th edition. Chicago: University of Chicago Press

ROMER, A.S. (1966) *Vertebrate Paleontology*, 3rd edition. Chicago: University of Chicago Press

ŠPINAR, Z.V. & BURIAN, Z. (1972) *Life before Man*. London: Thames & Hudson

SWINTON, W.E. (1970) *The Dinosaurs*. London: Allen & Unwin

TWEEDIE, M. (1977) *The World of Dinosaurs*. London: Weidenfeld & Nicolson

Some of the books listed above as published in London have also been issued by other publishers elsewhere, not necessarily in the same year. Some, moreover, are available as paperbacks and some in foreign-language editions.

Index